Aggression under the Guise of Liberation

Perry Pierik

AGGRESSION UNDER THE GUISE OF LIBERATION

The unnatural coalition between Hitler and Stalin and the Soviet invasion of Poland on 17 September 1939

Aspekt Publishers

AGRESSION UNDER THE GUISE OF LIBERATION
© Perry Pierik
© 2023 Publishing House ASPEKT
Amersfoortsestraat 27, 3769 AD Soesterberg, the Netherlands
info@uitgeverijaspekt.nl-http://www.uitgeverijaspekt.nl

Cover: Bob Hoegen
Interlining: Aspekt Graphics
Translated by: Isabel Oomen

ISBN: 9789464629989
NUR: 680

All rights reserved. No part of these pages, either text or image may be used for any purpose other than personal use. Therefore, reproduction, modification, storage in a retrieval system or retransmission, in any form or by any means, electronic, mechanical or otherwise, for reasons other than personal use, is strictly prohibited without prior written permission.

With the Soviet invasion of Poland on 17 September 1939, a secret and extraordinary pact became effective. Two opposing ideologies, National Socialism and Communism, joined forces to wipe the hated Poland off the map. Even plans for a sub-Poland were eventually dismissed. This cooperation had earlier historical roots, but was also born out of practical necessity.

Besides the origins of cooperation, we will reflect on the practical implementation of this pact. Europe's two largest armies fought the same opponent from opposite directions. With ideological diversity, conflicts and accidents lurked. Caution was imperative. Curiosity was also there; about each other's weapons systems, each other's armies and officers, and about the 'Jewish' political commissioners. Fear of friendly fire played a role as well, because accidents happen, and indeed things went wrong in several places.

In the end, the spoils had to be divided. What were the implications of September 17th? Who actually won the most, and how did things continue? The partition of Poland was the kick-off of a hugely complex military and historical event. So far, the Devil's Pact has attracted more diplomatic-historical interest than factual. Thanks to new sources, including the released Russian archives (with German material), this pact can now be charted in more detail for the first time. This victory was celebrated in Poland, but it was like dancing on a volcano; it ultimately did not allow itself to be smothered.

*

'Poland's real problem is geography', a journalist once wrote.[1] Polish-Russian relations have traditionally been problematic. Sandwiched in complex Central Europe - geo-politicologists spoke of the devil's belt[2] - Warsaw was caught between Western superpowers, especially the Habsburg Empire, (Napoleonic) France and (Nazi) Germany (Prussia) and the East, with the Tsarist Empire and later the Soviet Union. As a result, Poland was often a plaything of history. This was once again evident on 17 September 1939 when, completely unexpected, the Soviet Union invaded Poland. Poland had been at war with Hitler-Germany for more than two weeks by then, and this action accelerated the - already inescapable - Polish collapse.

The Polish campaign brought two irredentist regimes both alongside and opposite each other. The rapid German successes led Stalin to hastily invade Poland. The German side initially insisted on quick Soviet action, and then, when the German campaign went favourably and the Western Allies remained passive, they suddenly were particularly concerned about the future threat from Moscow. Cooperation and competition went hand in hand. Short-term interests were hidden behind the contrived peace. It would only last until the summer of 1941, when Berlin and Moscow clashed. The hardened pact, going back to the Treaty of Rapallo and the Weimar era, already entered a new phase on 17 September 1939, when the Soviet Union came to the aid of Nazi Germany and attacked Poland from behind.

History is a robust 'science'; 'Identität braucht Raum und Geschichte', the Germans sometimes say, which brings us straight to the heart of the problem. History often legitimises political actions and schools of thought and is thus an instrument of geopolitics.

Molotov-Ribbentrop Pact

In the current war between Russia and Ukraine, the weapon of history is being used again. The Akademie fur politische Bildung in Tutzing organised a seminar on today's tense Russian-Polish relationship[3] in April 2022. There, much attention was paid to the various historical perspectives. In collaboration with Polish historian

Joachim von Ribbentrop

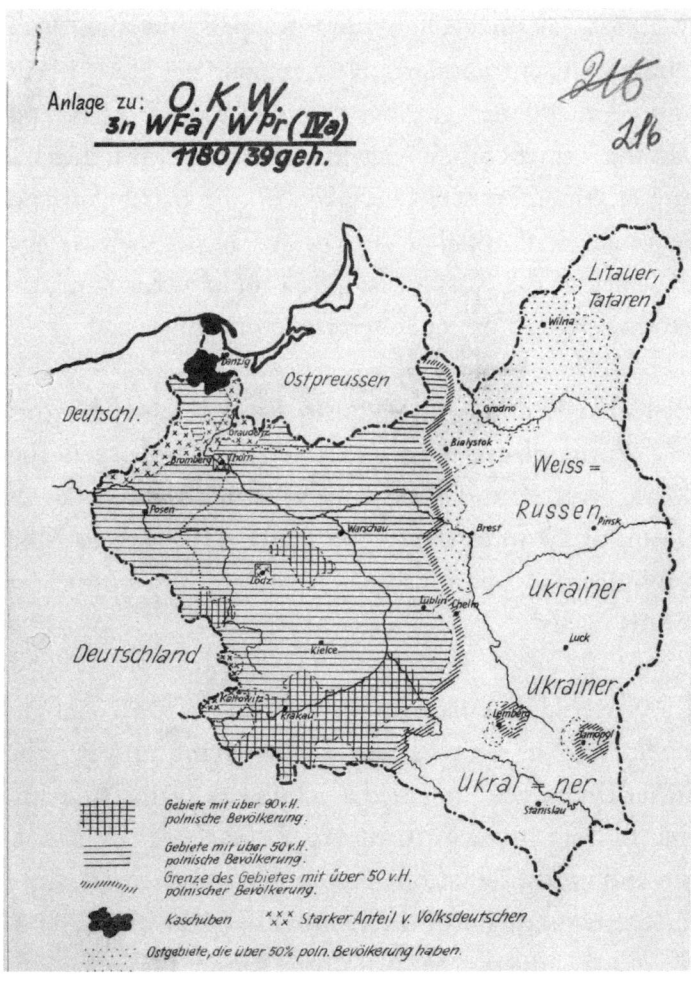

Etnic groups in Poland

Dagmara Jajesniak-Quast and Russian historian Vera Dubina, the current narrative was analysed. Here, it was noticed that Putin glorifies the old Soviet Empire and that the former empire is again important within the culture of remembrance. One plays on the patriotism and nationalism of Russian citizens, trying to increase the resilience of the Russian people. People in Kiev are also harking back to national heroism from the past.

Historian Dubina called Putin Russia's 'chief historian'.[4] Putin places Russia in the victim role, echoing World War II and the German attack on the Soviet Union of 22 June 1941. The many references to Nazi symbolism and politics in Ukraine are very important in this regard.

The Soviet Union played a glorious role in the 'Great Patriotic War' in which Putin is now trying to join. The Soviet Union was presented as a bulwark against Nazism, able to hold its own, thanks to the successes of 'socialism and industrialisation'. Perhaps for good reason, since the current struggle of the Donbas Basin involves one of the oldest industrial regions of the former Soviet Union. By anchoring the current struggle in the (glorious) past, Dubina argues, the costs and losses of the war are less important.[5]

Poland, which as a NATO and EU country welcomed millions of Ukrainians, also has its own narrative of how the conflict should be interpreted. Jajesniak-Quast emphasises that Poland sees itself above all as anti-communist, thus diametrically opposed to Putin's glorification of the Soviet Union. Since the fall of the wall, Poland has increasingly turned towards the West and obtained EU and NATO membership. Since 2015, and the rise of the PiS party, nationalism has become further fuelled and politically manifested. Traditionally Poland was in the victim role, victimised in the 20th century by Nazi Germany and the Soviet Union, but now the focus within the narrative has shifted to a more heroic view of the history of 'eternal Poland'.[6]

Molotov signs the pact

Incidentally, this narrative also has nasty sides, such as resurgent anti-Semitism in the 1990s, and that in a country practically devoid of Jews.[7] Furthermore, the sense of threat was always so great that Warsaw imaginatively

Maxim Litvinov

moved the security border far to the east.⁸ To prevent the worst excesses, all this resulted in 2018 in a law against Holocaust denial. The myth of Jewish-Bolshevism played a not insignificant role in the revival of anti-Semitism.⁹ The dialectical relations between Poland and Russia create constant verbal clashes between the two powers in the current conflict. It was not for nothing that Polish Prime Minister Mateusz Morawiecki warned of the impending Polish (NATO) - Russian clash as early as February 2022.¹⁰ On the Russian side, it was mainly the notorious Chechen Kadyrov who threatened Poland with war.¹¹

*

On the eve of World War II and the German invasion of Poland, German Foreign Minister Joachim von Ribbentrop arrived in Moscow. The German-Soviet rapprochement had been preceded by feints towards Poland. In January 1939, there had been intensive diplomatic contact between Berlin and Warsaw. In reality, both sides had secret agendas. Polish Foreign Minister Josef Beck was trying to tighten contacts with Moscow, while getting the Western Allies on his side. Hitler's eye was on the Soviet Union as well.¹²

The expansion of communism had gone through two phases in the Soviet Union since the 1917 revolution. The first phase was that of revolutionising the world, roughly running from the revolution to 1927, during

Vjatsjeslav Michajlovitsj Molotov

which the Soviets were fully active in bringing about revolutionary upheavals. The council republics in Hungary and Germany were part of this, as was the war against Poland, which stranded on the Vistula ('the miracle on the Vistula') opposite Pilsudski. Bulgaria and China followed as revolutionary operations. The second phase, in 1939 with Stalin, was the consolidation of power, with operations around communist ideology no longer through the permanent revolution, but through the Soviet Union itself. A claim to the old tsarist spheres of influence suited this, and was important with Poland in mind. In addition, Stalin zealously fought opposition in his own camp, especially that of the Trotskyists, who favoured an international approach.[13]

Von Ribbentrop's arrival heralded important talks that would go down in history as the Molotov-Ribbentrop Pact. For Berlin, the negotiations were of great importance and there was urgency: Hitler had already made his decision to attack Poland. He had 26 August in mind as the attack date, which was later pushed back to 1 September. Therefore, there was considerable pressure on Von Ribbentrop. Berlin thus sent the very man who was known as just about the biggest anti-communist in the Third Reich. Von Ribbentrop had endlessly pushed for the Anticominternpact, the league against communism, to which he also tried to persuade London. When all that failed, Von Ribbentrop changed his mind. He became an outspoken opponent of Britain and was persuaded by former Economy Minister Hermann von Raumer to take a more generous view of Moscow. The geopolitical and economic interests of

Nazi Germany and the Soviet Union were closer together than it seemed at first.[14]

The view was also clouded by a series of differences of interest, which played out in the Spanish Civil War, among others. In this conflict, fascist and communist ideology, dominant in the political game in Spain, were diametrically opposed.[15] For Berlin, helping Franco was also an attempt to stop communism in Western Europe. By late January 1939, the struggle had come to a head and a mass flight of the left from Barcelona took place, in an orgy of mutual violence. The egalitarian German press spoke of Soviet-Spanish tscheka massacres of anyone suspected of reactionary sympathies, right before the collapse of the anti-Franco front.[16] The fall of Madrid followed on 29 March and Franco joined the Anti-Comintern Pact on 17 April 1939. The tensions around Spain were not isolated. There were more difficult issues, such as the territorial disputes between Moscow and Tokyo in the east, where both the German-Japanese relationship and the relationship with the Kremlin had to be nurtured.

Von Ribbentrop, who arrived in Moscow on 23 August, had conversations with both Stalin and Foreign Minister Vyacheslav Molotov on the same day. However contradictory the regimes were, there was an important overlap in their interests. Both had been dependent on each other since the end of World War I due to their pariah status (defeated and revolutionised). Ever since the April 1922 Treaty of Rapallo, they had been cooperating (partly covertly) in various strategic areas. The journalist/historian John Toland rightly called the treaty an 'effective alliance'. Raw materials and technology, and weapons and machinery, were exchanged. The Red Army and Soviet industry could modernise while the 'black' (illegal) Reichswehr could circumvent the Versailles provision by still working on resilience at Soviet training grounds, such as mobile warfare exercises at Kazan.[17] In the 1939 situation, it was not only the partition of Poland that was important, but also the continued supply of strategic raw materials. An internal Heeres-Gruppenkommando 3 report of 22 August 1939 stated that the Berlin-Rome axis could hold out and resist British pressure (in the Balkans) as long as raw materials from the Soviet Union could be counted on.[18] Oil was particularly important in this regard. On an annual basis, Germany imported 0.84 million tonnes of petroleum (August 1939).[19]

The Western powers, London above all, reacted very rigidly to Rapallo at the time. From a British geopolitical point of view, fuelled by the ideas of Sir Halford Mackinder, who wanted to see the European continent divided by British supremacy at sea, they tightened the Weimar Republic's thumbscrews to such an extent that skyrocketing inflation was the result. As a result, the defensive alliance between the two countries ultimately did not last.[20]

This 'Ostpolitik', deployed by Chancellor Joseph Wirth and carried in German defence by General Hans von

Seeckt, already offered possibilities for action against Poland at the time. It was the originally Polish revolutionary Karl Radek who, in a personal conversation, suggested to von Seeckt that they move jointly against Warsaw. Von Seeckt and the Weimar administration wisely rejected these threefold plans at the time.[21]

By 1939, both regimes now sat much stronger in the saddle, and irredentist politics did its work. The Molotov-Ribbentrop Pact was above all about spheres of influence. Since this yielded immediate practical gains, they stepped over 'inconvenient details', such as the November 1936 Anti-Communist Pact, which, by the way, had been drafted to contain communism. Von Ribbentrop, not without humour, gave this a twist by stating that this pact was mainly 'against the West', which was not entirely untrue given his dislike of the British, and that therefore Stalin was allowed to join the pact as well.[22] Tensions between Moscow and Japan were brushed aside by Von Ribbentrop with the promise of diplomacy in favour of the Soviet Union, as was some distance from the Duce's outspoken anti-communism in Rome. Soviet demands towards strategic ports like Libau (Libava) and Windau (Vindava) were respectfully received.[23] All this happened miraculously shortly after Hungary's inclusion in the Anti-Comintern Pact. Political opportunism reigned supreme in Berlin and Moscow.[24] Moreover, both regimes had decided that the experiences of the Spanish Civil War, when the two

The Times on the 17th of September

countries in opposing camps had fought each other to the death, was water under the bridge.[25]

What both sides agreed on was the 'Polish question', with both Nazi Germany and the Soviet Union talking about 'Polish provocations'.[26] The talks eventually resulted in the infamous Molotov-Ribbentrop Pact, which in practice was a very short statement in which both sides promised not to attack each other, summarised in 280 words. Since 1947, we know that behind the official text were much larger agreements on the division of spheres of influence that covered several countries. This would directly influence the geopolitical playbooks of Berlin and Moscow. Among many other issues, this sealed the fate of Poland. The partition of central Europe thus became a fact.[27] With this, Poland fell between two stools for the umpteenth time in history. Nor was the bleak fate befalling Poland at

EASTER EGG COLORING.

On the propaganda of Stalin

all an exclusivity of Nazis or communism, but part of the bitter reality of state raison d'etre in central Europe. In the recent history before the Molotov-Ribbentrop Pact, in addition to Radek's and Von Seeckt's plans, a partition of Poland had already been an agenda item for Russian Foreign Minister Georgi Chichserin, who had advocated dividing Poland between the two superpowers during the 1926 neutrality treaty between Germany and the Soviet Union in Berlin. Had Gustav Stresemann (1878-1929) not then abandoned this initiative from Moscow, Poland's fate would have been settled under the Weimar regime.[28]

Even just before August 1939, there were signs that Nazi Germany and the Soviet Union were moving closer together. At the 18th party congress at the Moscow Bolshoi Theatre on 10 March 1939, Stalin made remarkably positive comments about Germany, dismissing rumours of German-Russian tensions as angry malicious slander.[29] It was the British and French who wanted to 'poison' the relationship between Berlin and Moscow, was the official view. The Soviet Foreign Ministry announced that yesterday's enemies had to become good neighbours. In addition, Stalin had taken an extraordinary step by sending his long-time trusted security adviser and foreign affairs commissioner Maxim Litvinov out of office. In his place, Vyacheslav Molotov was appointed. Stalin probably played on anti-Semitic sentiments in Berlin, forcing the Jewish Litvinov to make way for the big-Russian Molotov.[30] Added to this, Litvinow's wife, writer and translator, Ivy Teresa Low, was British, which could have been an obstacle too. The couple had met in London in 1915, and she, as a lover of Jane Austen's work, was far from an exemplary revolutionary. Her disinterest in communism and her love for Litvinov competed with each other.[31] That Molotov was in turn married to a Jewish woman, tailor's daughter Polina Zhemchuzhina, was apparently of less importance. For Stalin, that mattered; Molotov had been initiated into foreign affairs for years and immediately after taking office purged Litvinov's main backers, in good communist fashion. In doing so, he was pro-German, which was an advantage in light of the negotiations.[32] It was a remarkable gesture that, according to French historian A. Rossi, 'struck Hitler like a cannonball'. Hitler was said to have a certain admiration for the cold state raison d'etre of the Soviet regime.[33] That the Soviets attached importance to their decision to remove Litvonov from his position was shown by the fact that through Georgy Alexandrovich Astakhov, an employee of the Soviet embassy in Berlin, this message was personally conveyed to Karl Schnurre, the embassy's contact at the German Foreign Ministry, so the Germans could not miss the gesture.[34] Following that, a trade and credit treaty between Moscow and Berlin was signed as well on 19 August.[35] Polish historian Marek Kornat believed that with this decision, Stalin had abandoned the policy of 'Jewish-Bolshevism' and opted for 'national-communism'.[36]

In any case, it was clear that there was a special rapprochement. Historian Alan Weeks spoke of the Nazi-Soviet honeymoon.[37] The official position of Nazi Germany towards the Soviet Union was very positive. Hitler announced that he saw the Molotov-Ribbentrop Pact as an 'unprecedented political turning point' and that it was 'definitive'. Behind the scenes, he informed the Volkerbundkommissar für Danzig, Carl J.Burkhardt, that everything he did was 'directed against Russia' and that Germany needed the Ukrainian granary.[38]

*

Thus, the German invasion of Poland on 1 September 1939 did not come out of the blue. After thorough secret diplomatic preparations for the war, weapons now spoke. From the German point of view, Poland was almost the 'perfect' enemy. The Ost-Elbian Protestant-Prussian General Staff hated Catholic Poland, and the country was seen as an unnatural creation of the Treaty of Versailles.[39] Militarily, the German starting position was very positive for the Nazi's. Poland's location, and the way German forces could be draped around it, provided an excellent exit position for what August Gneisenau referred to as the 'Vernichtungsschlacht'. An all-decisive battle, therefore, from which the enemy could not recover. Although the battle was not a locally oriented battle, like, for example, the Battle of Waterloo, it mainly consisted of out-manoeuvring, disorientating, encircling and destroying the Polish army deployed on the borders.

This vulnerable positioning had everything to do with the Polish desire not to give up territory. Militarily and economically, they also had little chance, as Poland's important industrial areas, which were essential for modern warfare, were dangerously close to the border. Internal lines, especially railway lines, were also rather fragile. The best rail links were in the former Prussian areas of Poland and it was getting thinner eastwards. Rapid large-scale troop movements were therefore logistically very complicated.[40]

The geographical positioning meant that troops were in forward positions. The few important railway lines, Posen, Kutno, Warsaw, Cracow, Random, Deblin and Tarnow, Lemberg, would become a major target for Hermann Göring's Luftwaffe. Poland's total border with Germany, 5534 kilometres, was simply not defensible and, thanks to the disruptive depth attacks of the 'Blitzkrieg', the Polish army was soon knocked out of action. The attack followed a relatively simple concentric plan, where the main thrust came southwards from East Prussia and northwards from Silesia and smaller operations in the Carpathians. These major attacks, in the north commanded by General Fedor von Bock and in the south by General Gerd von Rundstedt, would result in major encirclement battles, roughly between Lódsch and Warsaw.[41]

The German attack was successful. The Luftwaffe managed to eliminate the Polish air force after bombing the airfields of Kattowitz, Kraków, Lemberg, Random, Tomaszow, Lodsch, Posen, Brest, Plock, Graundenz, Rahel and Puzig. This air superiority helped the mobile penetration of the German units. Communication points, bridges, troop concentrations were successfully attacked. This made an organised retreat impossible for the Polish troops. Carl von Clausewitz had pointed out this danger

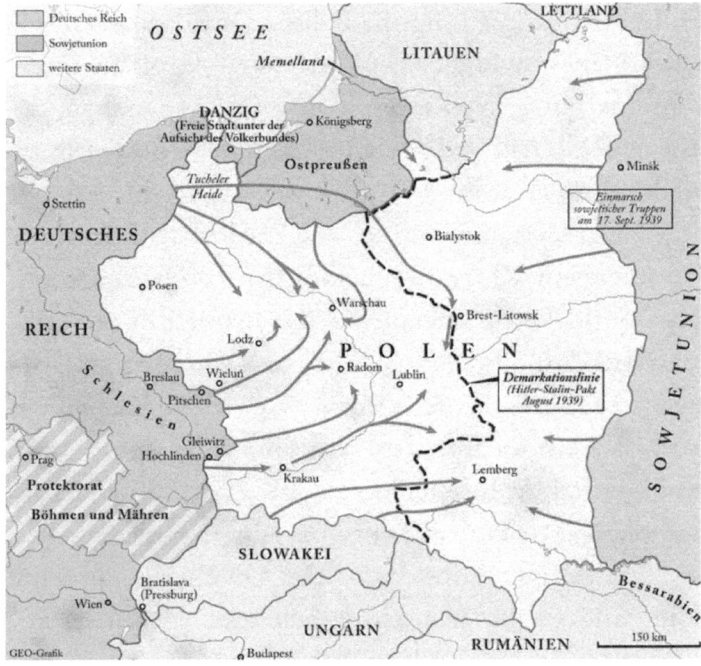

Poland 1939

in his famous military-philosophical work Vom Kriege. In the absence of cohesion, the Polish army did what any army would do in such a case. It became a disorganised flight, soon clinging to forests, fortresses and towns. At the river crossings in front of the destroyed bridges, vulnerable divisions carefully blended together. Militarily, the conflict was already decided after a week, although the fighting would continue for some time. But in the momentum itself, the Germans were not so sure of their case.

Hitler's attitude during the Polish campaign was modest. Hitler's biographer Ian Kershaw spoke of few interventions but a keen interest in military handiwork.[42] The generals still had a relative amount of power. Luftwaffe commander and Hitler loyalist from the very beginning, Hermann Göring, had clashed with General Gunther von Kluge just before the Polish campaign. The World War I veteran was commander of the German 4th Army operating in the so-called corridor between East Prussia and Danzig. Von Kluge had shown little concern for the party position of the vain Göring and ignored his interference. Göring had subsequently complained to Hitler about Von Kluge. Hitler showed his displeasure to the staff. The OKH, the supreme command of the army, had then rejected Hitler's request to replace Von Kluge. When battle broke out and Von Kluge performed well, Hitler withdrew his criticism. In fact, when the general dropped out for some time due to a plane crash on 4 September, Hitler was very worried.[43]

Hitler followed the war from the so-called Führer train, with the 'Truppenübungsplatz' Gross Born in Pomerania as its home base. From there, German divisions were regularly visited via so-called 'Frontfahrten', which was a security nightmare for the German officers responsible for Hitler's safety. With a platoon of motorcyclists and armoured cars, Hitler ventured through uncleared areas, where there was still Polish cavalry. The later Afrika Korps general Erwin Rommel, in the rank of Oberst, was in charge of the dangerous ritual.⁴⁴

Hitler's involvement in the war also stemmed from concern. The Nazis were not entirely convinced of the success of the 'Blitzkrieg' strategy beforehand. After all, it was a new military concept, which had to be proven on the battlefield. As late as 7 September, when in hindsight the battle was actually already won, Hitler was still considering a peace with Poland and the creation of a Polish hull (residual) state. The latter was also part of the secret clause of the Molotov-Ribbentrop Pact, at least insofar that the possibility of a buffer state was left open. However, Hitler's ideas around 7 September may also have been motivated by uncertainty about the front course and the possible plans of Paris and London.⁴⁵

The unrest came mainly from the fact that the invasion of Poland had eventually resulted in a war with Britain and France on 3 September. According to historians Weissbacker and Patzold, Hitler had seen the Western powers' guarantees towards Poland mainly as part of the political poker game and war of nerves that preceded the battle as a tactical weapon. In doing so, he went against the advice of his own confidantes, who believed that London and Paris would support Poland. In certain German circles, there was the idea that the Western Allies also understood well that the Polish corridor could not hold in the long run and that there was therefore a certain 'legitimacy' in

German action. The Nazi historian Helmut Sundermann, for example, had expressed himself along these lines, citing the British minister Lloyd George, who had argued as early as 1919 that the Polish corridor would lead to war.[46] Now that the Western powers had put their money where their mouth was by declaring war, a dangerous situation had arisen for Germany.[47]

There were now growing tensions in the West and it was important to avoid a potentially active two-front war. Speed was of the essence. To hasten the Polish collapse, Berlin invoked its secret arrangements with Moscow and urged Stalin's help soon after the invasion of Poland. On 29 August, Von Ribbentrop had informed the Soviets that war could 'break out at any moment'. Thus, the attack had come as no surprise. That same day, Rome was also informed by the Foreign Ministry through Ambassador Bernardo Attolico.[48]

On 3 September, Von Ribbentrop asked Molotov when to expect the Soviet invasion. Molotov held off, stating that 'the time was not yet ripe'.[49] The Kremlin was also working through the German ambassador to Moscow, Friedrich-Werner Graf von der Schulenburg. Five days later, on 8 September, another German request for intervention came. It was clear that people on the German side were extremely tense. Pressure on Moscow was mounting. Shortly before the German invasion, in late August, there had also been tensions. The Western press had reported that the Soviets had withdrawn their troops on the Polish border. This meant that Warsaw could focus entirely on Germany, and, if this was true, would the Soviets attack at all? When Foreign Affairs asked about these rumours through Ernst von Weizsacker and Ambassador Schulenburg, Molotov burst into laughter. According to him, there was no time to 'bother with all these rumours'. Still, the suspense had been serious since, on 30 August 1939, Moscow took the precaution of officially distancing itself from these rumours in the party newspaper Tass.[50]

The Kremlin followed developments closely, and saw that the German Wehrmacht was making tremendous progress. The Western Allies stood Gewehr beim Fuss on the border, and did not intervene. Stalin was surprised by this development, and Molotov informed Von Schulenburg on 9 December that military action would be taken one of these days. Internally, Stalin admitted to being surprised by 'the rapid successes'.[51] On 14 September, at least something happened on the paper front. The party newspaper Pravda published a large front-page article sharply attacking Poland and questioning the existence of the state. The reason Moscow cited was the treatment of the country's ethnic minorities. Moscow was already working to account for the coming invasion.[52]

*

What caused Stalin's slow response? The most logical explanation is that the Kremlin simply wanted to see which way the wind would blow. After all, Germany was now at war with Paris and London, and for all they knew, the war could be taking an entirely different turn. The inaction of the Western powers and Germany's rapid advance made it clear that there would be no last laugh; Moscow had to secure its secretly negotiated territories. On 16 September, only a day before the invasion, Stalin gave the final green light.[53]

What received relatively little attention, but which undoubtedly occupied the Kremlin's mind intensely, were simultaneous Soviet operations in the border region of Mongolia. A territorial dispute between Japan and Russia led to growing tensions there. This had already led to hostilities at Lake Chasan in 1938, and in May 1939 Japan carried out an expansionist operation with the so-called Kanto-Gun army. On the border with the Mongolian People's Republic and Japanese-occupied Manchuria, an undeclared war had broken out between Japan and the Soviet Union. Initially, it had been limited infantry pinpricks and - mainly - air battles, such as over Lake Buir-Nur. Although the Soviet air force resisted, that did not discourage Tokyo from gathering troops near the Chalchin-Gol river.[54]

Moscow had sent one of their best generals, Georgi K. Zhukov, to the threatened People's Republic just before the Japanese operation. Zhukov, who was to play an important role in World War II, was deputy commander of

Soviet forces in Belarus when he was summoned to Moscow on 1 June 1939. There he was ordered to avert the danger and on 5 June, Zhukov arrived in Tamzak-Bulak, where the local Soviet headquarters was located.

The case focused around the Chalchin-Gol river. The Soviets bombed the bridges and the 11th Soviet Panzer Brigade, commanded by M.P. Jakavlew played a special role. In a pre-Blitzkrieg-like manner, this unit overran the Japanese army by attacking the Japanese from the movement and concentrically. Soviet BT-5 and BT-7 tanks were tested here in combat and perfected after the battle. The attack took place by surprise, on a Sunday, knowing that many Japanese officers were on leave. Great chaos was the result. Japan's 6th army was 75% destroyed in these battles. Tokyo's losses amounted to 61,000 men in killed, wounded and missing, and they also lost 660 aircrafts. This was offset by 26,000 Soviet losses, and 249 lost aircrafts.[55] As a result, Japan abandoned the 'northern' (land war) strategy towards Siberia and opted for the southern (naval war) thrust towards the Pacific. The importance of this decision cannot be overstated.[56] Due to the Japanese defeat, delegations from the Mongolian People's Republic, Japan and the Soviet Union met on 15 September 1939 and an armistice was signed the next day. Moscow had its hands free for its operations in Poland. The new peace between Moscow and Tokyo resulted in a non-aggression pact between the two countries in April 1941, despite Von Ribbentrop's attempts to thwart this initiative.⁵⁷

The successful conclusion of the battle in the east paved the way for action against Poland. Moscow could now safely assume that the Western Allies would not make too great an effort to intervene. An internal OKH report on the German side made it clear that French artillery in particular was active on the western front, but that apart from probing the German defences and reconnaissance operations, major attacks were lacking. Only around the town of Pillingen, near the Luxembourg- French border, had heavier fighting occurred, but even there the battalion level was not reached. The German rapporteurs therefore reported that there was still little to say about the combat value of the French army.⁵⁸

The German advance into Poland was going well. By 16 September, the so-called Kessel of Kutno was almost complete. Large numbers of Polish troops were trapped here, and these were units of as many as five different Polish army corps (III.de, X.de, XIth, XIIIth and XVIth). German intelligence officers had established that these were units of some 16 divisions, with divisions of cavalry units including the Pomorska and Nowogrodzka brigades.⁵⁹ Here and there, the situation was already transitioning from front area to military administration, such as in the city of Bialystok, where on 18 September the commander of Feldkommando 581 was appointed military administrator of the city. He took up residence in the building of a Polish bank. Polizei Battalion 6 guarded order in the city.[60]

In addition, the Germans were concerned about the fate of the Volksdeutschen in Poland, with the Bromberg massacre receiving much attention. The day before the Soviet invasion, an internal German report had appeared on the Bromberg issue. In the small town of the same name, violence had broken out against Volksdeutschen on 3 and 4 September 1939, killing many. The perpetrators were largely Polish soldiers. Charred and mutilated corpses lay in the streets and the issue was used to justify the invasion.[61]

*

On 17 September, news finally arrived that the Soviet Union had invaded eastern Poland. Commanded by General Timoschenko and General Kowalew, several Soviet armies - totalling 750,000 men, divided into 25 infantry divisions, 16 cavalry divisions and 12 armoured and mechanised brigades - crossed the border. The Poles were numerically no match, and the best units in western and central Poland were also fighting the Germans. In eastern Poland, there were few regular units and they mainly had troops in training, garrison and border units. In practice, this made the 1400-kilometre-long border virtually

Sovjet cavalerie september 1939

Soviet BA-10 in Poland

indefensible, with about 10 soldiers per linear kilometre. Moreover, there was a lot of confusion on the Polish side. Some Soviet units carried white flags with them, as if they were 'coming to the rescue' of the Poles. Polish historian Mieczyslaw Bielski spoke of 'deceptive propaganda tricks'.[62] There were salutes here and there. Polish officers urgently requested instructions from their own headquarters, which was also confused and on the run.

Polish commander Edward Rydz-Śmigły ordered to avoid the battle and to flee to neighbouring countries.[63] Nevertheless, some considerable fighting occurred, at Grodno on 21 and 22 September and at Koddziowcanti. In both cases the Soviets suffered heavy losses, including material (tanks). In well-equipped positions, the Poles in the Polesie region held out for days. Fitted with anti-tank weapons, they inflicted heavy losses on the Red Army. Polish units with a strength of some 7,000 men, commanded by General Wilhelm Orlik-Riickeman, fought at Ratno and Shatsk, with some success.[64]

Luftwaffe intelligence reports on the day of the invasion said: 'Strong Russian units crossed the Polish-Russian border in full width between Kamemnez-Podolskii and Polozk'. According to the Luftwaffe, the operation was proceeding well, as Soviet cavalry units would penetrate as much as 50 kilometres into Polish territory that first day. In southern Poland, the Germans reached the demarcation line with the Soviet Union near the Seret River.[65]

Soviet 'liberators'

The German-Soviet arrangements were mainly a pact and not a true friendship. German intelligence therefore closely followed the Red Army's every move, although good relations were paramount for the moment. Thus they got hold of Soviet pamphlets that were dropped, such as over the Polish units trapped around Bialystok. The text, drafted by the commander of the Soviet Belarusian front, Michal Kowalow, bluntly announced that the Polish 'aristocratic-bourgeois government' that had 'plunged Poland into adventure' had been overthrown. 'The great and invincible Red Army', Kowalow continued, would bring the working class a 'fraternal and happy life'. Poles were freed from the sphere of interest of 'tycoons and capitalists'. The Soviets would also end the oppression of Belarusians and Ukrainians.⁶⁶ Ambassador I.M. Maiksi articulated Moscow's position in his memoirs. The Soviet invasion came as a 'salvation' for Belarusians and Ukrainians living on Polish soil. The Polish government no longer existed, and in this sense the Soviets created 'order and authority'.⁶⁷

The official statement, issued by Molotov, was equally sinister. Moscow claimed that the raid was caused by 'events', and was necessary because 'nobody knew where the Polish government was'. Naturally, Soviet 'state security' was invoked and had to intervene to protect western Ukraine and western Belarus. Not a word about their own responsibility in creating the conflict, which had taken shape in the secret agreements of the Molotov-Ribbentrop Pact.⁶⁸ Protecting Belarusians and Ukrainians was a typical Soviet interpretation of reality as well. The Soviet Union, even during the Cold War, liked to present itself as an anti-imperialist freedom movement, but in practice it was working for the Soviet empire. The (national) interests of Ukraine and Belarus were certainly not paramount, and de facto Moscow fought against any form of Belarusian or Ukrainian autonomy. The murder of Ukrainian leader - in exile - Yevgen Konovaletsy on Coolsingel in Rotterdam on 23 May 1938, was bloody proof of this, as was the policy towards Stefan Bandera, who followed in Konovaletsy's footsteps.⁶⁹ The Soviet declaration had been handed over to the Polish ambassador in Moscow. The next day, 18 September 1939, the declaration was published in Izvestiia ('Messages'), a Soviet newspaper founded in 1917.⁷⁰ A week earlier, Comintern contacts and agents had already been instructed to act against Poland. Bulgarian Komintern leader Georgi Dmitrov - known in the West for the Reichstag-fire trial - announced that 'the destruction of this country [Poland] under favourable conditions would mean one less bourgeois fascist country'.⁷¹

Beyond studying pamphlets and speeches, Berlin was also interested in what Soviet liaison troops had to report. Overheard messages were received and analysed by, among others, the 'Horchabteilung Nord', based in Köningsberg. There was a lot of activity. On 21 September, the Chef des 'Heeresnachrichtenwesen' reported that they had now mapped 123 Red Army 'Funkstellen'. This showed that the Soviets reported a good reception among the population (probably among the Belarusian and Ukrainian minorities) who stood by the roadside with flowers. Historian Jan T. Gross argued that there was Soviet infiltration by agents on the eve of the invasion who had prepared a good reception. Local militias were actively helping to forcibly mobilise the population to give the Soviets a positive reception.⁷² The first military successes were reported as well, including 500 to 600 prisoners of war and captured Polish trucks. From 17 September onwards, the Germans tried to get a picture of the size of the Soviet units, counting some six corps that had crossed the border from Belarus (17th

, 2nd, 5th , 14th 18th and 60th (Kav.) corps) and the independent regiments 25 and 33, the latter two units of which would soon meet Polish resistance. Near Nemerinzy, fighting ensued. On 18 September, at 0325, it was called: 'the enemy flees into the forest'.[73] By 19 September, the Red Army had reached the Wilna - Lida - Wolkowysk - Brest - Luck - Lember - Stanislau - Kolomyja line with strong units.[74] By 21 September, the picture was much more complete and more units came into view, including armoured units, such as the Xth Tank Corps, and the 11th , 15th , 22nd and 25th tank brigade. One also sometimes caught not uninteresting details, such as the 4th Schutzen-Division, which had 'no meat and no fuel'.[75]

*

By no means all ethnic Ukrainians and Belarusians welcomed the Soviet invasion of eastern Poland. Like Poland, the Soviet Union was an opponent of autonomy efforts for Ukraine and Belarus. Ukrainian nationalist Stephan Bandera, who was in Polish captivity in 1939, was kept behind bars by Moscow after the fall of Poland. The Nazis would free him in 1941, only to arrest him again after declaring Ukrainian independence on 30 June 1941.[76] A flood of refugees began to appear and these civilian men were immediately questioned by the German army's military intelligence about the image they had gained of the Soviets. The army diary of the

Captured polish tanks

14th army, part of Heeresgruppe Süd, reported that this gave an 'interesting' picture of the atmosphere and morale in the Red Army.[77] The flow of refugees would only increase in the following days. On 21 September, the IVth Army Corps reported an 'unprecedented amount of refugees' on the east-to-west road on Chelm-Piaski street. According to this report, the main motive of the refugees was fear of the Red Army.[78] That same day, a secret document of the XVIII Army Corps, signed by General Konrad, revealed that now that the Soviet Union had invaded, Poles and Jews who had crossed the demarcation line to the east while fleeing the German army should no longer be allowed to flee to the west. The Volksdeutschen, on the other hand, had to be supported in their attempts to come west.[79] The Swedish press was already reporting arrests in Soviet-occupied Poland on 22 September.

A large series of practical measures were immediately issued on the German side, as there was great fear of incidents that could jeopardise the relationship. Orders went out that if the German and Soviet troops were going to meet around the demarcation line, it was imperative that the German officers should immediately greet their Soviet counterparts and that the soldiers should show comradeship.[80] Units on march in eastern Poland were also ordered to provide their troops and vehicles with clear swastika flags so that 'friendly fire' would be prevented as much as possible.[81] Additionally, a large number of Russian interpreters were rushed to the units. Acting as umbrella 'translation officers' were Major Nagel for the German 4th army, Dr Spalcke for the 3rd army, Kretschner for the 10th army and Von Heygendorff for the 14th army. Officers were also exchanged via airfields St Rus, Stok, Bialaczow and Rudna, in order to coordinate the operations of both armies in an increasingly smaller playing field.[82]

For Poland, the disaster was now complete. The Polish government evacuated to Romania that day, and Hitler forbade the evacuation of the Polish civilian population from Warsaw. The capital became increasingly surrounded. At the Modlin fortress, Polish units were trapped; the war was preparing for its final bloody phase.[83] Polish

The Wehrmacht in Warsaw

civilians were also trying to flee the country; a German intelligence report of 20 September cited 10,000 refugees to Romania and 50,000 to Lithuania.[84] Some 70,000 civilian and military personnel had fled across the Carpathians and ended up in Hungary. Among the armed units that managed to escape were the troops of Polish generals Milian Kamski and Stefan Dembinski.[85]

Furthermore, the latter battles saw bitter fighting between Polish units commanded by General Wladyslaw Anders, who carried with him a large number of German and Soviet prisoners in addition to his own troops. It was a surreal sight. The group broke through towards Sambor and managed to reach Hungary.[86]

*

While measures were running to best coordinate the operations of the Wehrmacht and Red Army, things went wrong on the 19th. According to the war diary of the German 14th army, in the front area of the Heeresgruppe Süd a firefight between Soviet troops and German troops occurred on the eastern edge of Lemberg (Lwow). On the 17th, Von Blumentritt had immediately warned his units of the Soviet invasion of Poland. The message had been transmitted first by radio, and later in writing. In doing so, immediate measures were taken to prevent skirmishes and 'friendly fire'. Thus it was proclaimed that the 14th army should not cross the Skole - Lemberg - Wlodzimierz line eastwards.[87] Nevertheless, it came to a clash two days later. This involved a 'Pak-Sperre' (an anti-tank gun position) of the German 2nd mountain division, which clashed with two Soviet armoured vehicles. The German division had moved east towards Grodak after the encirclement of Lemberg by the 1st Geb D., the 7th Pz.D. and Pz.Rgt.15, after which the incident took place. On the German side, one officer was killed and several soldiers were wounded. The OKH was on top of the matter and later informed the 14th army that the 2nd mountain division was 'in its right'. To avoid further trouble, Oberstleutnant Von Blumentritt announced at 1100 the next day that Hitler had ordered that the town of Lemberg be handed over to the Red Army.[88]

By then, the last of the Polish army's resistance was collapsing. There was still some organised resistance around Modlin and Warsaw, but other than that there was very little cohesion in the Polish defences. The 213th German infantry division, part of the German 8th army, reported from the Orlow and Tarnow area - part of the front around Kutno where regiments 354, 406 and 318 were active - that more and more Polish soldiers were trying to escape home - in civilian clothes.[89] General Von Kleist announced in his corps order (XXII Army Corps) on 19 September that the troops 'after incessant forward storming' had fulfilled their mission.[90] Indeed, the units' day orders at that time were mostly filled with the proper interpretation of positioning along the line of demarcation between the German army and that of the Soviets.

An order from the 14th army under General List and part of General Von Rundstedt's Heeresgruppe Süd stated that the demarcation line had been established along their front section as follows: The border ran 2 kilometres east of Czorna Repa - Olszanoweo - Czyrak - Magura - Matachin - Neu Mudy - Opor Bach at Skole - Mikolajow, so road and railway remained west of the demarcation line - Zubrza-Bach - Lemberg - Kamionka - Strumilowa and further along the banks of the Bow River. Two cleared towns, Sokal and Wloddzimierz, had been wrongly cleared and had to be reoccupied.[91] All in all, it was an ingenious cartographic poker game that had to be executed accurately.

On 20 September, the German supreme command, through Von Brauchitsch, officially proclaimed the end of the battle of the Weichselboog, which began at Kutno. It was referred to as a 'Siegeslauf'. Heeresgruppe Süd specified its successes by declaring the end of the Battle of Lódz with 120,000 Polish lives lost. General der Kavalerie Erich Hoepner (later with the Resistance) addressed his troops from the XVIth Army Corps and suggested that 'the first part of the war was won', thereby indicating the situation on the western front. 'Nach dem Siege binde den Helm fester', he informed his troops, including the 1st and the 4th Panzerdivision and Hitler's elite unit the 'Leibstandarte Adolf Hitler'.[92] Historian Georg Soldan retrospectively divided the campaign into five phases. From 1 to 5 September, the battle of the border positions took place, followed by 6 to 8 September, the defeat of the Polish field troops. Between 9 and 14 September, the encirclement battles took place and between 15 and 20 September, the destruction of the encircled units. From 21 September to 5 October, the battle for Eastern Poland took place. 694,000 troops were made prisoners of war. By 27 September, Warsaw had fallen.[93] Several units announced victory earlier, such as General Kriebel of the 56th I.D. of the Southern Army Group, which was deployed near the town of Przemysl.[94]

The trick now was to unravel the various troops again around the demarcation line. From the XVIII Army Corps, Oberts i.G. Hofmann, Oberstleutnant Von Heygendorff and Rittmeister Buerklin were deployed to achieve the separation along their front section.⁹⁵ The fact that the Germans had sometimes lost material of strategic significance, which now laid on the terrain east of the demarcation line, was complicating matters. The German high command urgently indicated that these weapons had to be secured and taken away, which was easier said than done. In case of heavy damage, a 'Nachkommando' had to stay behind to protect the strategic weapon from prying eyes of the Red Army, at great risk.⁹⁶

Danger lurked everywhere. Things had gone wrong at Lemberg before, and when the town capitulated to German mountain troops, the last German shell fell on the town at noon, while Soviet troops were entering Lemberg from the east at that time. General Kubler, of the German 1st Geb.D. did proudly report that the Polish capitulation was caused by German efforts before the Russians arrived.⁹⁷

Lemberg was a major (railway) hub and the city had attracted the soldiers of the mountain division like 'a magnet'.⁹⁸ Kubler had deployed his fiercest units, a Kampfgruppe led by the 'bat-hearted Hund' Ferdinand Schorner, who was building a notorious reputation as a ruthless commander. His unit, consisting mainly of

Front near the city of Lemberg

troops from regiment[98], had advanced to Lemberg via Sambor, as part of the XVIII. Geb.korps. The unit had been in such a hurry that they had run out of ammunition and had to fight their way forward with captured weapons and cartridges. The Ia of the division, Max Pemsel, later recalled that it was a pity that the town had to be handed over to the Soviets, as many graves of fellow soldiers were now on the eastern side of the demarcation line. The division had lost 1402 troops during the Polish campaign.[99]

'All along the eastern front encounters are taking place,' Heeresgruppe Nord reported on 22 September. Where the Germans were to fall back to the west, it was agreed that the Red Army would keep a distance of 25 kilometres when following units westwards.[100] At the end of the day, an initial report came in from Hofmann, Von Heygendorff and Burklin on the encounter between German and Soviet units. They had met the Soviets with white flags attached to their vehicles. They were immediately stopped and surrounded and officers and political commissars came to watch. It was clear that the Red Army was insufficiently aware of the joint advance against Poland. 'We encountered partly mistrust, hostility and disbelief,' the trio reported, 'at an artillery regiment and a corps command we were received more kindly'. 'We believe the Jewish commissars, whom we met at some units, showed less interest in connections'. Where the Germans were received by staff, the contact was 'correct but distant', which Hofmann in his report traced back to 'the presence of Jewish commissars'. On their way to the staff, the German officers were accompanied by a Soviet armoured car, and passed Russian soldiers who threatened to shoot at them because they were believed to be Poles. In Podborce, Hofmann and his colleagues were eventually able to do business with the Soviets, asking them to 'treat Germans and Ukrainians well'. The Soviets made commitments and indicated they would report this to Przemysl on 23 September through liaison officers, where there was a contact point. Finally, Hofmann, Von Heygendorff and Burklin did mention that the Soviets made a good impression in terms of discipline, weapons and horses. The officers were generally 'deutschfreundlich', while the commissioners, insofar as they were Jewish, were dismissive.[101]

Soviet troops, photographed by the 1.Gebirgsdivision in Lemberg

In another von Heygendorff report, the commissioners came off slightly better. During a discussion between officers of the German XVIII Corps and a Russian colonel, the commissioner informed that Germany's position in the east was secure because of the pact between Berlin and Moscow: 'Ehrenwort ist Ehrenwort'.[102]

Major i.G. Nagel of the 206th I.D. reported contact with several political commissars from Friedrichshof on 26 September. One of them, Rykow, he got to know a bit more personally, but the contact was businesslike and distant. Rykow was 35 years old and made an intelligent impression. Names of senior officers were not shared. Nevertheless, Nagel managed to get the name

Meeting between the Germans and the Red Army

Cooperation between Germans and Russians was complicated

of the serving Russian officer in his report, Semjonoff, who commanded the troops around Bialystok. 'Reticent, suspicious, a proletarian type,' Nagel noted about the colonel in his report. He also observed Soviet armoured units. Nagel saw the familiar tanks with 3.7 and 4.7 cm guns. The trucks with grenadiers did not make the best impression. The vehicles were overstaffed with 16 men and formed a motley crew of different types. Most were old and worn out. The major's final conclusion about the Red Army was: 'reluctant and repellent, one does not extend the same courtesy as we do. Distrustful and secretive about their own plans and units. The troops are young but their uniforms are nowhere near as neatly groomed and disciplined as ours.'[103]

*

Establishing the demarcation line was easiest where waterways formed the divide. It was mutually agreed that the Germans should stand west of the Pisia on 28 September, on the 30th west of the Narew, west of the Weichsel at Bedlin on 3 October and on 4 October at Pultusk on the Narew.[104] The process was sometimes disrupted by unexpected actions of the Polish army, which still sometimes struck surprisingly large. On 23 September, this resulted in cooperation between the Soviet Red Army in Lemberg and the German forces west of it. Via a Ferschreiben, the 14th army announced that the Soviet commander in Lemberg, General Iwanoff, was warning of large-scale

Polish attacks westwards. This would involve three divisions and cavalry units that also had strong artillery units. The attack was expected from the Tomaszow, Tyszowce - Rzezyca area. The 14th army could take advantage of this information and urged the Soviets to exert pressure from Lemberg towards Mosti Wielki - Belz in order to throw the Polish troops off balance.[105]

Less fortunate was an encounter between units of the 10th German Pz.D. of the XIX Army Corps and Soviet cavalry units. On 23 September, a firefight occurred just north of the town of Widomla. Units of the Aufklärungs Abteilung (A.A.) 8 were approached in their armoured car by some 20 horsemen who opened fire. In response, the Germans fired back. These were Soviet troops. Here, too, the German authorities were on top of things. Through interrogations of participants, such as Emanuel Cieslok from the town of Hindenburg, the incident was weighed and judged. As early as 24 September, there was a report absolving the German unit of guilt. It had come to the incident because many Polish cavalry attacks had previously taken place, the attack came unexpectedly from a northern direction, while the Soviets had until then approached from the east and the Soviets had fired first. In doing so, the Poles and Soviets, the Ia of the 10th Pz.D. noted, had very similar uniforms. The matter was taken up on the spot with the Soviet officer on duty. There were two casualties on the Soviet side. There were no German losses.[106]

At that point, the Germans could also infer less from the Soviet radio messages overheard. On 24 September, the eavesdropping unit in Allenstein reported that there was much less radio traffic than before; especially from the armoured units and cavalry. From this the Germans concluded that the Red Army had met the marching targets. Most radio traffic at that time was from infantry units carrying out purge operations.[107] In general, it became clear that the Soviets were moving forward in eastern Poland. Newspapers were already reporting in Ukrainian and White Russian to clarify the Soviet position. The Moscow press reported extensively on the war in Poland and the demarcation line with Germany.[108]

Indeed, the Soviets were serious about imposing their system on the Poles, just as they were, at the same time, stepping up pressure on the Baltic states and later towards Bessarabia and Romania. The German ambassador Schulenburg was once again summoned to Stalin on 25 September, and the Kremlin made it clear to him that, as far as Moscow was concerned, no Polish rump state should remain. Such a creation would only generate turmoil and seek to play out Germany and the Soviet Union against each other.[109] Meanwhile, in the field, the Soviet embassy in Warsaw was evacuated. The 62-strong staff had been trapped there since 17 September, and were in the basement of the badly damaged building. Among them were more than 20 children. All of them could now leave the city under German guidance.¹¹⁰ As the Soviet diplomats left, a German spy ('Vertrauens')-Mann reported that barricade fighters in Warsaw, affiliated with the Socialist Party, were eagerly awaiting the arrival of the Red Army. They hoped for communist solidarity in the struggle against the Nazis. Unfortunately such hopes were a pipe dream. Warsaw was lost, despite the numerous barricades in the city. There was hunger, disease and a lack of everything.¹¹¹

The surrender of the Polish capital Warsaw came on the same day the embassy was evacuated. The commanding Polish general Rommel accepted the German terms. Some 120,000 troops in the city capitulated. A day later, the fortress of Modlin fell. German General Bohme of the 32nd I.D. took command of the Polish fortress.¹¹² The division of the spoils was complete, although difficult detailed questions remained. Through the 57th I.D., for example, a curious report came in on 6 October. Relations with the Soviets on the San River were good, although even here people complained about the political commissars. However, east of Bakligrod on the San River was the Raiskye oil field, as well as 50,000 kg of crude oil. The latter was in the German section, but the oil derricks were east of the demarcation line. Major Schmidt, assigned to the 57th I.D. asked for guidelines on how to proceed.¹¹³

*

Burining village at the front

Along the advance route

Traces of War

Surrender at Modlin

The results on the ground were politically confirmed by a new agreement between Berlin and Moscow, through the German-Soviet Border and Friendship Treaty. The question of a Polish rump state was now off the table: Poland no longer existed. Initially, Stalin too seemed to feel for a residual Poland, as a 'buffer' against Nazi Germany. Yet with Poland's rapid collapse, Stalin seemed to abandon this option.[114] The demarcation line had been announced to the outside world in a joint communiqué from 22 September, and on the 23rd Von Ribbentrop had expressed his willingness to once again sit down with Stalin and Molotov to discuss remaining issues. Preparatory work took place with German ambassador Schulenburg, who was at the Kremlin on 25 September. On September 28th, the German-Soviet border and friendship treaty was signed. We know from preserved notes by Schulenburg's associate Gustav Hilger that the talks with Molotov were very friendly and in high spirit. Von Ribbentrop could report that the war in the West had still not really erupted and spoke smugly of a 'Kartoffelkrieg'. Up until now, Von Ribbentrop claimed, not one French pilot has dared to fly across the German border.[115]

Some final practical matters were settled. A small area swap took place on former Polish territory to smooth the demarcation line between Berlin and Moscow. This formed the core of the border and friendship treaty. Still, Stalin also had his eye on the Baltic States, where there was an immediate claim towards Lithuania (Moscow

Disarmament of the Polish Army

end of the Estonian nation-state. On 3 October, Schulenburg reported that the Lithuanian foreign minister had been summoned to Moscow. Here, the framework of the 'mutual assistance treaty' would be discussed. The Soviet claim on Lithuania was a lot to take in for Berlin. Germany saw Lithuania within its sphere of influence and as a border country within the so-called four-river line, Pissa-Narew-Weischsel-San.[117]

*

The German negotiating position with the Soviet Union was strong due to successes in Poland, but not optimal. The still ongoing war in the West naturally played a role. Nevertheless, it was easier to remain friends when dividing gains than when dividing losses, and Von Ribbentrop's performance finished with endless toasts to countries and leaders. The most important question for Germany was asked on the second day of negotiations with Stalin. What was Moscow's position on Romania? Stalin initially kept a somewhat low profile on this, stating that he had no immediate intentions of interfering with Romania. Given that he also pretty much said the same about the Baltic States and, meanwhile, was effortlessly intimidating these countries and bringing them within his own sphere of influence, the Germans must not have been sure.

Welcome to the Red Army

Stalin and Lenin are introduced to the Polish people

In terms of oil, Nazi Germany depended to a not insignificant extent on the oil fields of Romanian Ploiesti. However, Stalin's irredentist policy towards Romania would eventually play enormously into Berlin's strategic hands. Through Moscow's diplomacy of simply claiming Bessarabia from Romania in 24-hours time in June 1940, Bucharest was driven directly into Berlin's hands. Although Germany protested against the action via Schulenburg in Moscow, there was nothing they could do due to the Molotov-Ribbentrop Pact. In it, Germany had indicated that Bessarabia was not within the German sphere of influence. This gave Moscow the green light.[118]

*

Moscow again added thousands of square kilometres of land to the already infinite empire, but the oil treasures of Ploiesti fell into German hands, when Romania, after a change of government through Marshal Ion Antonescu, came to seek shelter with Berlin against its big neighbour. Bucharest stepped over the antipathy towards Horthy Hungary -since the Treaty of Trianon and border changes the great enemy in the region- and invited the German 'Heeresmission' to guard the oil fields of Ploiesti. This greatly strengthened the grip on Romanian oil. Even in the days leading up to the Polish campaign, Bucharest had delivered extra oil to Poland to upgrade its strategic reserves.[119] Now the oil could work for Germany. With

Antonescu, Hitler secured his greatest ally during World War II. This brotherhood of arms would last until August 1944, when the Soviet breakthrough into Romania took place and Antonescu was overthrown. He would end up before the firing squad.[120]

Soviet-occupied eastern Poland, eight provinces, which historian Jan Gross referred to as 'Poland-B', an area of 201,000 km2, fell apart economically and was exploited by Moscow. Soviet policy was strongly ethnicised. The area, in which before the war 37.7% of Poland's population had lived (13.2 million inhabitants) consisting of 5.2 million Poles, 4.6 million Ukrainians, 1.2 million Jews and 2.2 million White Russians and others, faced unruly politics. The lion's share of these people lived in rural areas, 81%, while the national average was 72%. A quarter of the population was illiterate.[121]

On the face of it, Ukrainians and Belarusians (see annex) benefited, and there initially was a positive response among some of them to the Soviet occupation. Their language became officially recognised and prevalent in the school system. In some places, political commissars literally appealed to the population to retrieve their property from their class enemies, killing them if necessary. Yet, there was also distrust from Moscow towards the nationalist tendencies of these populations, which did not fit into Soviet thinking. Repression was the cornerstone of Soviet policy.[122] Poles were at the very bottom of the hierarchy. Jews, who often formed the middle class in the cities, fell victim to nationalisation of their shops and factories, and in the countryside land was confiscated. Even the communists suffered under Soviet occupation. There was distrust towards the pre-war top of the Polish Communist Party. These were ousted from top positions and replaced by people loyal to Moscow. Several waves of deportations also took place, totalling 900,000 people. Poland was deprived of the most resilient part of its population. Among them many officers from the Polish army, who later, 15,000 to 17,000 strong, were found murdered in the forests near Katyn and other places. In practice, almost 11% of the population of the Soviet part of Poland was in a labour camp or in prison by 1941.[123]

*

Soviet losses in the Polish campaign have always remained somewhat obscure. On 31 October 1939, Molotov himself reported that the Soviet Union suffered 737 killed and 1862 wounded, but historian K. Liszewksi put the figure at between 2,500 and 3,000 killed and 5,000 to 7,000 wounded. That was the balance of 21 months of Soviet rule until the summer of 1941.[124]

While in the eastern part of Poland the Soviet secret service NKVD struck, the western part of Poland was occupied by Nazi Germany. Here, too, it was doom and gloom. The 'Reichsgauen' Danzig-Westpreussen and

Wartheland were separated from Poland, and between Warsaw and Kraków the so-called Generalgouvernement was created. In the September days, Jews had already fallen prey to 'Blitzpogrome'. Their case would now become structurally worse and led to the infamous concentration camps. The Polish population was as exploited as in the Soviet zone.

On 7 October 1939, Hitler announced the so-called 'Erlass zur Festigung deutschen Volkstums'. This document focused entirely on German 'Volksgruppenpolitik'. The idea was to classify and treat Central - and Eastern Europe in particular - according to population groups, with the Germans, of course, as the 'organising element'. In practice, this not only paved the way for far-reaching repression, but also for the 'Lebensraum' field trip to the east. The 'Generalplan Ost', detailing how the conquered territory was to be ruled and enslaved, was worked out. As a result, the armed peace that prevailed in conquered Poland could never be of a permanent nature.[125]

German losses were considerably higher than those of the Red Army. Some 15,000 German soldiers had been killed and over 30,000 wounded.[126]

Thus, German-Soviet cooperation ended in a new constellation of power that would trigger a new war in June 1941. Until then, the pact had endured. A pact that had come into being in August 1939, and which had been a fragile rapprochement during the Polish campaign. Drunk on victory, the cake had immediately been cut further, and, beyond the Baltic States and Bessarabia, the Soviet Union would even attack Finland. Nazi Germany plunged into the Balkans and Greece after the Western campaign. The map was cut up again until there was nothing left to cut up. Then two pacting powers faced each other. It was a long road to Operation 'Barbarossa'.

Notes:

1. Don Graff, Poland's real problem is geographie, In: *Gadsden Times* 22.12.1981.
2. Authors Friedrich List and Friedrich Naumann pointed at the 'peoples dungeon' of Central Europe. See chapter 1.2, Midden-Europa, in: Perry Pierik, *Karl Haushofer en het nationaal-socialisme. Tijd, werk en invloed*, Soesterberg: uitgeverij Aspekt 2006, p. 28 e.v.
3. For a report of the seminar see: Sophia Maier, *Die instrumentalisierung der Erinnerung. Wie Russland und Polen die eigene Geschichte lenken.* 04-04-2022 website Akademie für politische Bildung te Tutzing.
4. Ibid.
5. Ibid.
6. The phrase 'The everlasting Polen' was used by Peter Michielsen.
7. Perry Pierik/Marcel Reijmerink, Rechts lonkt naar de macht in Polen, In: *Algemeen Dagblad* 24.06.1993/Perry Pierik/Marcel Reijmerink, Lech Walesa speelt dubieuze rol in aanloop verkiezingen, In: *Haagsche Courant* 24.08.1993.
8. Perry Pierik, Polen voelt zich belegerd. In: *Elsevier* 04.04.1992.
9. Over de mythe van het Joodse zie Arkady Vaksberg, *Stalin against the Jews,* New York, Random House 1995

10 Michael Backfisch/Sebastian Vannier, *Polens Ministerpresident warnt vor Angriff auf Nato*, WAZ 27-05-2022
11 Tschetschenenführer Kadyrov droht Polen mit Krieg. *Blue News* 27-05-2022
12 John Toland, *Hitler, Het einde van een mythe*, Utrecht: A.W.Bruna, 1983, p. 561/Dr. Kleist, Ribbentrop auf Staatsbesuch in Warschau am 26 Januar 1939 in: *Der Weg*, Mai 1949, p. 87-91.
13 Malcolm Mackintosh, *Stalin's Policy towards Eastern Europe, 1939-1948. The General Picture.* p.230-232.
14 Michael Bloch, *Ribbentrop*, London/New York: Bantam Press 1992, p. 233,234.
15 On the ideological element in the Spanish civil war, L.H. Grondijs, *Spanje,een voortzetting van de Russische revolutie?* Soesterberg: Uitgeverij Aspekt 2016. The original printing was from 1937.
16 'Massenflucht aus Barcelona. Nationale Geschütze beschiessen die Stadt', In: *Baruther Anzeiger* 25.01.1939
17 Toland, p. 564
18 Heeresgruppenkommando 3, Ubersicht über die politische Lage, Berichtszeit 21 und 22.08.1939, Bestand 500, Findbuch 12464, Akte 92.
19 Geheim! Oberkommando der Wehrmacht, Nachrichtenblatt Wehrwirtschaft UdSSR Nr.1 25.08.1939, NARAT311/R244
20 Mauricio Metri, *From the Rapallo Treaty to War in*

Ukraine: the western Policy Towards Moscow-Berlin Relations. Strategic Culture Foundation, April 15, 2021. For more of Mackinder's line of thought see o.a. Perry Pierik, *Hitlers Lebensraum. De geestelijke wortels van de veroveringsveldtocht naar het oosten* (later republished as *The Geopolitics of the Third Reich*), Soesterberg: Uitgeverij Aspekt 1999, chapter 2, De Schreibtisch-veroveraars. See also: Karl Haushofer, *Weltpolitik von heute*, Berlin: Zeitgeschichte Verlag Wilhelm Anderman, 1934, chapter 13. For the positive impact on Soviet industry of German-Russian cooperation, see Bogdan Musial, *Stalins Beutezug. Die Plünderung Deutschlands und der Aufstieg der Sovjetunion zur Weltmacht*, Berlin: List Verlag, 2011, pp. 42-55. For Rapollo's influence on Germany see o.a. Franz von Gaertner, *Die Reichswehr in der Weimarer Republik. Erlebte Geschichte Darmstadt.* Fundus Verlag 1969 / chapter F, John W. Wheeler-Bennett, *The Nemesis of Power. The German Army in Politics 1918-1945*, London: Macmillan 1954, p. 83 e.v.

21 Rabenau, F. von, (hg.), Seeckt, *Aus seinem Leben*. Leipzig: Von Hase & Koehler Verlag, 1941, p. 309

22 Emerson Vermaat. *Het Ribbentrop – Molotov Pact 1939. De prelude op de Tweede Wereldoorlog*, Soesterberg: Uitgeverij Aspekt, 2005, p 53. Japan also later put a spin on the Pact from political interests that would be 'anti-communist' but not 'anti-Russian', see *Wat is Anti-Komintern? Niet 'Anti- Rus-*

sisch' zegt Tokio, In: Algemeen Handelsblad voor Nederlandsch-Indië 03.02.1940.
23 Ibid. p.53
24 The signing by Hungarian foreign minister Stephan Csaky took place on 24 February 1939.
25 Carr labelled the years 1936-1937 as the 'height of frenzy' between Berlin and Moscow, In: Edward Hallett Carr, *Germany-Soviet Relations between the two World Wars, 1919-1939* Oxford; Oxford University Press 1952, p. 117.
26 Vermaat, p 53.
27 This so-called 'Geheimen Zusatzprotokoll', a secret additional protocol, was also dated 23 August 1939, although the actual signing took place on 24 August 1939, Vermaat. p.55. Alan Weeks spoke of 'carving up the world' in relation to the division of spheres of influence. Albert L. Weeks, *Stalin's other war. Soviet Grand strategy 1939-1941*, Langham New York Rowman & Littlefield Publishers, Oxford 2002, p.75
28 Ibid. p 57
29 Bernd Bonwetsch spoke of an undisguised attack on Western powers. Bernd Bonwetsch, *Vom Hitler-Stalin-Pakt zum 'Unternehmen Barbarossa'. Die deutsch-russischen Beziehungen 1939-1941 in der Kontroverse.* In: Osteuropa. Zeitschrift für Gegenwartsfragen des Ostens. 41.Jahrgang/Heft 6/Juni 1991.
30 Richard Overy and Andrew Wheatcroft called Mol-

otov a 'Soviet nationalist'. R.Overy & A.Wheatcroft, *The Road to War*, London: Vintage, 1989, p. 210.

31   Brigid O'Keeffe, *Madame comrade. How Ivy Litvinov, the English-born wife of a Soviet ambassador, seduced America with wit, tea and soft diplomacy.*

32   Toland, p.569/Weeks, p.70/Overy/Wheatcroft, p. 210. Geoffrey Roberts has pointed out that there was also party criticism of Litvinov's recent political actions , which may also have played a role in Stalin's decision. See: Geoffrey Roberts, 'The Fall of Litvinov: A revisionist View'. In: *Journal of Contemporary History London/Newbury Park/New Delhi* Vol. 27 1992.

33   Cites to John Toland, p. 569 referring to note 16 page 1045, A.Rossi, *Deux ans d'alliance germano-sovietique,* Parjs 1947 p. 27

34   Office of the Historian. *Foreign Relations of the United States, 1949, Eastern Europe: The Soviet Union, Volume V* The Director of the Policy Planning Staff (Kennan) to the Counselor of the Department of State (Bohlen), Frankfurt, March 15 1949.

35   Heeresgruppenkommando 3, Ubersicht der politische Lage, Berichtszeit 19. und 20.08.1939, Bestand 500, Findbuch 12464, akte 93

36   Marek Kornat, *Pakt Ribbentrop-Molotow, Interpretacje, mity, rzeczywistosc*, Institut historii Polskiej Akaddemii Nauk, 2020

37   Albert L Weeks, *Stalin's other War. Sovjet Grand*

Strategy 1939-1941, p.85/Robert Conquest, *Stalin, Breaker of Nations*, London: Weidenfeld, 1993, p. 220 e.v.

38   Krummacher/Lange p. 392,393/Bernd Bonnwetschargues that on that day, the Soviets definitively opted for cooperation with Nazi Germany after breaking down negotiations with the Western powers. Bernd Bonwetsch, *vom Hitler-Stalin-pakt zum 'Unternehmen Barbarossa'. Die deutsch-russischen Beziehungen 1939-1941 in der Kontroverse*, In: Osteuropa, Zeitschrift für Gegenwartsfragen des Ostens, 41.Jahrgang/heft6/juni 1991, p.568.

39   See chapter 'De Pruisische haat tegen het katholieke Polen,' Perry Pierik. *De Poolse oorlog een ambitieus Warschau gevangen tussen de grootmachten*, Soesterberg Uitgeverij Aspekt 2020 p. 35 e.v.

40   See Kurze wehrwirtschaftliche Uebersichten (Ausland) GDIR Akte 9)/Ausarbeitung des Oberkommandos der Wehrmacht, Die Wehrwirtschaft der Republik Polen Teil 1 vom 10 Juni 1939 GDIR Akte 26

41   Pierik, *De Poolse Oorlog*. p. 161

42   Ian Kershaw, *Hitler 1936-1945 Nemesis*, London: Pinguin Books (2001) p 236

43   Nicolaus von Below, *Als Hitlers Adjudant 1937-1945*. Mainz: Von Hase & Koehler Verlag 1980. P. 205.

44   Pierik. *De Poolse Oorlog*. p. 228, 229.

45   Ibid. P. 177

46 Helmut Sündermann, *Die Gezeichneten. Tatsachen über die Schuldigen des Zweiten Weltkrieges*. Berlin: Zentralverlag der NSDAP 1945, p.9

47 Kurt Patzold/Manfred Weissbecker, *Adolf Hitler. Eine politische Biographie*, Leipzig: Militizke Verlag 1995, p.384. There was perhaps more reticence from Foreign Affairs than from the military camp. These refrained from advising on war or no war, but it was clear that British and French military commitments to Poland for the autumn of 1939, especially in terms of arms supplies, would not in practice be met. By now this had become clear, leading to great disappointment on the Polish side. It was also concluded that Moscow was not supplying arms to Warsaw, confirming serious Soviet intentions regarding the Molotov-Ribbentrop Pact. See: OKH, Geheim! Die militärische Lage in Polen am 12.08.1939, NARA T311/R236. In een Lagebericht van 17.08.1939 stated that the Western powers were, on the one hand, trying to get Poland's back, and on the other, were looking for a peaceful solution. The problem, however, was that both Paris and London could no longer offer workable proposals and compromises. In: Heeresgruppenkommando 3, Ubersicht über die politische Lage Berichtzeit 17.08,.1939, abgeschlossen 18.08.1939 In: GDIR Bestand 500, Findbuch 12464, Akte 93.

48 Bloch p. 255

49 Krummacher/Lange p. 393
50 Jan T. Gross, *Revolution from Abroad. The Soviet Conquest of Poland's Western Ukraine and Western-Belorussia*, Princeton/New Jersey: Princeton University Press 1988 p, 8-9.
51 Vermaat, p. 60.
52 Final Report to National Council for Soviet and East European Research. Jan Gross, Russian Rule in Poland, 1939-1941, 14 July 1984 p. 6
53 Weeks, p. 73.
54 Georgi K. Schukow, *Erinnerungen und Gedanken*, Stuttgart: DVA 1969, p. 150 e.v.
55 Albert Axell, *Marshal Zhukov. The Man who beat Hitler*, London/New York: Pearson/Lomngman, 2003, p.61.
56 https://www.military.com/daily-news/2019/08/27/japan-strikes-north-how-battle-khalkhin-gol-transformed-wwii.html
57 Otto Preston Chaney, *Zhukov*, Oklahoma University Press 1971 p.74/Rudolf Bohr, *Stalins rugdekking. Japan en het Molotov-Ribbentrop Pakt* In: *Intermediair* 25e annual issue 33, 18 August 1989.
58 OKH-Heeresgruppe B, Beobachtungen über Kampfverfahren der frz.Truppe seit dem 16.9.39 In: GDIR Bestand 500-Findbuch 12454-Akte 3.
59 Heeresgruppe Nord Auszug aus Fernschreiben OKH, Abt.Fremde Heere Ost 16.09.1939 In: GDIR page 62851.

60 Armeebefehl für die Herstellung u. Erhaltung der Ordnung in Bialystok, 18.09.1939 in: Bestand 500, Folder 12472, Akte 151-0014.
61 Betr. Fernschreiben HZNH Nr. 186 HNCHG 1063 16.09. 12.40 Uhr. Geheim! Mit richterlicher Untersuchung der Vorgänge in Bomberg Beauftragter Ob.Kriegsgerichtrat meldet: NARA T354/R609
62 https://repozytorium.ukw.edu.pl/bitstream/handle/item/5611/Wojna%20polsko%20sowiecka%201939.pdf?sequence=1&isAllowed=y. Mieczyslaw Bielski, Karol Liszewski (pseudonim:Wojna polsko-sowiecka) 1939.p2
63 Ibid.
64 Ibid.
65 Der Oberbefehlshaber der Luftwaffe-Luftwaffe-Führungsstab Ic Lagebericht Ost nr.29, 17.09.1939 In: GDIR: Bestand 500, Findbuch 12452-Akte 72.
66 Übersetzung des von einem russischen Flieger über Bialystock abgeworfenen Flugblattes, 17.09.1939, GDIR Bestand 500, Findbuch 12459-Akte 20-0022
67 I.M.Maiski, *Memoiren eines sowjetischen Botschafters*. Berlin: Dietz Verlag 1973, p.522.
68 Rede des Vorsitzenden des Rates der Volkskomisare der S.S.S.R. Genossen Molotoff [spelling in document] vom 17.09.1939, GDIR: Bestand 500, Findbuch 12459, Akte 20-0031. For the 'lib-

eration myth' see also Sergej Slutsch, 17.September 1939. Der Eintritt der Sowjetunion in den Zweiten Weltkrieg, In: *Vierteljahrshefte für Zeitgeschichte, 2000, Heft 2*

69   Perry Pierik, *Met Hitler voor moedertje Rusland. De geschiedenis van patriottistische Sovjetcollaborateurs*, Soesterberg: Uitgeverij Aspekt, 2022, p. 30 e.v. 30ff. The importance attached to quelling everyone's Ukrainian aspirations for autonomy was also underlined by the fact that it was agent Pavel Sudoplatov who liquidated Konovalch with a bomb. Sudoplatov had also been entrusted with the murder of Leon Trotsky in Mexico and was a top Lavrenti Beria agent.

70   Edward D.Wynot Jr., *World of Delusions and Disillusions: The National Minorities during World War II*, Cambridge University Press 20.11.2018.

71   Marek Kornat, *Pakt Ribbentrop-Molotow, Interpretacje, mituy, rzeczywistosc*, Institut historii Polskiej Akaddemii Nauk, 2020.

72   Jan T.Gross, p.4

73   Horchabtlg.Nord, Funklagemeldung Nr.2 Königsberg 18.09.1939, GDIR: Bestand 500, Findbuch 12459, Akte 28-0041.

74   Der Oberbefehlhaber der Luftwaffe, Luftwaffeführungsstab Ic, 19.09.1939 GDIR, Bestand 500, Findbuch 14252, Akte 77.

75   Der Chef des Heeresnachrichtenwesens, Horchleitstelle,Nr. 2682/39g, Horchlage Ost, Ber-

lin 21.09.1939, GDIR: bestand 500, Findbuch 12472, Akte 145-0015.

76 Bandera hoped Ukraine could follow the example of Tiso in Slovakia or Pavelic in Croatia. Perry Pierik, *Met Hitler voor moedertje Rusland. De geschiedenis van patriottistische Sovjetcollaborateurs*, Soesterberg: Uitgeverij Aspekt, 2022 p. 34 ev./Per A. Rudling, The OUN, the UPA and the Holocaust. A Study in the Manufactering of historical Myths In: *The Carl Beck Papers in Russian & East European Studies* Number 2107 University of Pittsburgh zj. Yves Bizeul (hg.)., *Rekonstruktion des Nationalmythos? Frankreich, Deutschland und die Ukraine im Vergleich*, V&;R Unipress p. 231.

77 KTB AOK 14 , Darstellung der Ereignisse, 22.09.1939, GDIR: Bestand 500, Findbuch 12468, Akte 10-0048.

78 (barely readable)[…] Ia. Bericht: Am Generalkommando IV.A.K. 21.09.1039, GDIR: Bestand; 500, Folge 12474, Akte 65-0015.

79 Kommandostab XVIII, Geheim! Den 21.09.1939, GDIR: Bestand 500, Findbuch 12474-Akte 272-0259.

80 Fernschreiben an H.Gr.Nord 17.09.1939 GDIR: Bestand 500 Findbuch 12459,Akte 20-0004. This order was passed down to company level, possibly beyond. See: (2.)Panzer Division, Divisionsbefehl (most likely 18 September) GDIR: Bestand 500, Findbuch 12478, Akte 15-0007.

81　Fernschreiben an H.Gr.Nord /H.Gr.Süd 17.09.1939 GDIR: Bestand 500, Findbuch 12459, Akte 20-0006
82　OKH PA/GZ Nr.145 17.09.1939 GDIR Bestand 500, Findbuch 12459, Akte 20-0009
83　Von Below,p.205/Czeslaw Madajczyk, *Die Okkupationspolitik Nazideutschlands in Polen 1939-1945*, Koln: Pahl -Rugenstein 1988 p.7
84　Der Oberbefehlshaber der Luftwaffe, Luftwaffenführungsstab Ic, Lagebericht Ost Nr. 32 20.09.1939, GDIR: Bestand 500, Findbuch 12452, Akte 77.
85　Endre B. Gastony, *Hungary and Geopolitics. The Second World War and the Holocaust 1938-1945*, Soesterberg: Uitgeverij Aspekt, 2019, p. 30. On the Polish units, see Bielski, https://repozytorium.ukw.edu.pl/bitstream/handle/item/5611/Wojna% 20polsko%20sowiecka%201939.pdf?sequence=1&isAllowed=y.
86　Ibid.
87　KTB AOK14, 17.09.1939 GDIR: Bestand 500, Findbuch 12468-Akte 10-0029
88　KTB AOK 14, 19.-20..09.939, GDIR Bestand 500, Findbuch 12468, Akte 10-0031,0032/ Der Oberbefehlshaber der Luftwaffe-Luftwaffe-Führungsstab Ic Lagebericht Ost nr.29, 17.09.1939 In: GDIR: Bestand 500, Findbuch 12452, Akte 72.
89　213.I.D. Befehl für die Abriegelung des Gebietes

beiderseits Kutno gegen flüchtende poln. Militär in Zivil, Div.St.Qu. den 18.09.1939, GDIR, bestand 500-Findbuch 12477, Akte 106-0106.
90   Kommandierende General des XXII.A.K., te Siedliska, Korpsbefehl 19.09.1939, GDIR: bestand 500, Findbuch 12478, Akte 15-0011.
91   Armeekommando 14, Ia Nr. 131/39 A.H.Qu. Rzeszow Befehl 18.09.1939, GDIR Bestand 500-Findbuch 12477, Akte 446-0053, which units were specifically concerned here, see: Friedrich Stahl, *Heereseinteilung 1939*, Eggolsheim; Dorfler-Verlag z.j. p. 170 e.v.
92   Generalkommando XVI.A.K., Korpsbefehl 20.09.1939, NARA T354/R609.
93   Perry Pierik, *De Poolse oorlog. Nieuwe feiten rond diplomatie, onderdrukking, oorlog, spionage en slachtofferschap*, Soesterberg: Uitgeverij Aspekt, 2021 p. 166, 302
94   56.Infanterie Division, Div.St.Qu.Przemysl, 22.09.1939, GDIR: Bestand 500, Findbuch 12477, Akte 446.
95   Der Kommandierende General, Das XVIII. Armeekorps, Ermächtigung zu Verhandlungen mit der russischen Kommandostelle, 22.09.1939, GDIR: Bestand 500, Findbuch 12474, Akte 272.
96   OKH berichet in: Anlage KTB Heeresgruppe Süd, Kielce 21.09.1939, NARA T311/Roll244.
97   1.Gebirgsdivision -Kommandeur-An die Truppe ist Folgenden bekanntzugeben, den 22 Septem-

ber 1939, GDIR: Bestand 500, Findbuch 12474, Akte 272.
98 Excerpt from Hauptmann Helmuth Grashey, quoted from Hermann Frank Meyer,, Blutiges Edelweiss. Die 1.Gebirgs-Division im Zweiten Weltkrieg. Berlin: Ch.Links Verlag 2008, p.28
99 Ibid.p. 28-30
100 Fernschreiben H.Gr.Nord-geheime Kommandosache 22.09.1939, GDIR: Bestand 500, Findbuch 12464, Akte 83-0034.
101 Korpskommando XVIII, Meldung über die Fühlingsnahme mit dem russischen Korpskommando bei Lemberg (Podborce) am 22.09.18.00 Uhr, GDIR: bestand 500, Findbuch 12474, Akte 272-0293.
102 Bericht über das Zusammentreffen mit dem Russen zwischen Przemysel und Lemberg 26.09.1939 in: GDIR: Bestand 500, Findbuch 12474, Akte 272-0214.
103 Major i.G.Nagel, Ia. 206 Division, Div.St.Qu.Friedrichshof: betrf.: Beobachtungen bei Berührung mit russ. Truppen 26.09.1939 GDIR: Bestand 500, Findbuch 12459, Akte 209
104 H.Gr.Nord, Allenstein 22.09.1939 23.00Uhr. GDIR: Bestand 500, Findbuch 12459, Akte 24-0036.
105 Fernschreiben A.O.K.14 23.09.1939 Bestand 500, Findbuch 12474, Akte 272-0260.
106 An die 10.Panzer Division, Bestand 500, Findbuch

12478-Akte b82-0020/10.Panzer-Divison Abt. Ia Div.St.Qu. den 24.09.1939: Betr: Zusammenstoss zwischen russ. Streitkräften und der A.A.8 am 23.09.1939 Bestand 500, Findbuch 12478, Akte 82-0022.
107 Fernschreiben HDIH 884 an H.N.F. Allenstein und H.Gr.Nord 23/24.09,1939 GDIR: Bestand 500, Findbuch 12459, Akte 29-0022.
108 Nachrichten. Deutschl.-Sender 12.30 Uhr 24.09.1939, NARA T354/R609.
109 The German Ambassador in the Sovjet Union (Schulenburg) to the German Foreign office, telegram 25.09.1939 published in: *Nazi-Soviet Conspiracy and the Baltic States. Diplomatic Documents and other Evidence.* London: Boreas Publishing Co. 1948 document 26 p. 37,38/Discussion Von Ribbentrop and Stalin in late September 1939 in Ingeborg Fleischhauer, Der Deutsch-Sowjetische Grenz-und Freundschaftsvertrag vom 28 September 1939. Die deutsche Aufzeichnungen über die Verhandlungen zwischen Stalin, Molotov und Ribbentrop in Moskou, In: *Osteuropa. Zeitschrift für Gegenwartsfragen des Ostens*. 41.Jahrgang/Heft 6/ Juni 1991. p. 458.
110 Sowjetbotschaft verliess Warschau. Durch deutsche Hilfe befreit. In: *Bayreuther Zeitung* 27.09.1939.
111 Fernschreiben, Geheim 25.09.1939 GDIR: Bestand 500 Findbuch 12464, Akte 83-0028.
112 Armee Oberkommando 8 A.Gef.Stand Gradziek

27.09.1939 Armeebefehl NARA T354/R609.
113 Major Schmidt, Telephonische Meldung, 06.10.1939, Bestand 500 Findbuch 12474, Akte 272-0052.
114 Ibid., p.451
115 Fleischhauer, p. 453.
116 *Nazi-Soviet Conspiracy*, Doc. No.29 Secret Supplementary Protocol, p. 39.
117 Letter Von Ribbentrop to Schulenburg, 5.10.1939, In: Nazi-Soviet Conspiracy, Doc. 35 The Reich Foreign Minister to the German Ambassador in the Soviet Union (Schulenburg) p.43 For the Baltic States, Soviet interference was the start of repression, murder, imprisonment and deportation of large parts of the population. In Estonia, for example, out of a population of 1.1 million, 47,000 people were arrested for political reasons, 35,000 deported and thousands executed. See: Olaf Mertelsmann/Aigi Rahi-Tamm, *Soviet Mass Violence in Estonia revisited*, In: *Journal of Genocide Research* (2009) 11, June-September p. 307-322.
118 Perry Pierik, *Wapenbroeders. Roemenië, nazi-Duitsland en operatie 'Barbarossa'*, Soesterberg: uitgeverij Aspekt 2021, p.36 e.v.
119 This would involve 3,000 wagons of oil. Oberkommando der Wehrmacht, Betr. Wehrwirtschaft Polen, *Nachrichtenblatt Wehrwirtschaft Polen Nr.3* 11.08.1939 NARA T311/R244.
120 Pierik, *Wapenbroeders*, p. 123 ev.

121 Gross, p. 4-5.
122 Patrick E. Campbell, Jr., *What would be the Harm? Soviet Rule in Eastern Poland, 1939-1941*, August 2007, p.11-12.
123 Gross, p 4-5. Antony Polonsky, *Stalin and the Poles 1941-7*, In: European History Quarterly Vol. 17 (1987) p. 454.
124 See also Robert Blobaum, *The Destruction of East-Central Europe, 1939-41* in: *Problems of Communism*, Nov. Dec. 1990 p. 106 e.v. Bielski. https://repozytorium.ukw.edu.pl/bitstream/handle/item/5611/Wojna%20polsko%20sowiecka%201 939.pdf?sequence=1&isAllowed=y
125 Erlass des Führers und Reichskanzlers zur festigung deutsches Volkstums, 7 Oktober 1939, In: 1000dok.digitale-sammlungen.de
126 Pierik, *De Poolse oorlog*, p.270 ev. en p.302. e.v.

Literature:

Axell,A., Marshal Zhukov. *The Man who beat Hitler*, London/New York: Pearson/Longman, 2003,

Backfisch,M./Vannier,S., *Polens Minister president warnt vor Angriff auf Nato*, WAZ 27-05-2022

Bielski,M., Karol Liszewski (pseudonim) : Wojna polsko-sowiecka 1939

Bizeul,Y., (hg.), *Rekonstruktion des Nationalmythos? Frankreich, Deutschland und die Ukraine im Vergleich*, V&R Unipress p. 231.

Blobaum, R., The Destruction of East-Central Europe, 1939-41 in: *Problems of Communism*, Nov.Dec. 1990

Bohr,R., *Stalin's rugdekking. Japan en het Molotov-Ribbentrop Pact* in: Intermediair 25e volume 33, 18 August 1989.

Bonwetsch, B.,Vom Hitler-Stalin-pakt zum Unternehmen 'Barbarossa'. Die deutsch-russischen Beziehungen 1939-1941 in der Kontroverse, In: *Osteuropa, Zeitschrift für Gegenwartsfragen des Ostens*, 41.Jahrgang/Heft6/juni 1991

Below,N.von., *Als Hitlers Adjudant 1937-1945* Mainz: Von Hase & Koehler Verlag 1980

Bloch,M., *Ribbentrop*, London/New York: Bantam Press 1992

Campbell, P.E. Jr., *What Would Be the Harm? Soviet Rule in Eastern Poland, 1939-1941*, August 2007 (thesis)

Carr, E.H., *Germany-Soviet Relations between the two World Wars, 1919-1939* Oxford; Oxford University Press 1952

Chaney, O.P., *Zhukov*, Oklahoma University Press 1971

Fleischhauer, I., Der Deutsch-Sowjetische Grenz- und Freundschaftsvertrag vom 28 September 1939. Die deutsche Aufzeichnungen über die Verhandlungen zwischen Stalin, Molotov und Ribbentrop in Moscow, In: *Osteuropa. Zeitschrift für Gegenwartsfragen des Ostens.* 41.Jahrgang/Heft 6/June 1991

Gaertner, F.von., *Die Reichswehr in der Weimarer Republik. Erlebte Geschichte*, Darmstadt: Fundus Verlag 1969

Gastony, E.B., *Hungary and Geopolitics. The Second World War and the Holocaust 1938-1945*, Soesterberg: Aspekt Publishers, 2019

Graff, D., *Poland's real problem is geographie*, In: Gadsden Times 22.12.1981

Grondijs, L.H., *Spanje, een voorzetting van de Russische revolutie?* Soesterberg: Publisher Aspekt [1937] 2016

Gross, J.T., *Revolution from Abroad. The Soviet Conquest of Poland's Western Ukraine and Western Belorussia*, Princeton/New Jersey: Princeton University Press 1988.

Haushofer, K., *Weltpolitik von heute*, Berlin: Zeitgeschichte Verlag Wilhelm Anderman, 1934

Kershaw,I., *Hitler 1936-1945 Nemesis*, London: Penguin Books, 2001

Kleist, Ribbentrop auf Staatsbesuch in Warsaw am 26 Januar 1939 in: Der Weg, Mai 1949.

Kornat,M., *Pakt Ribbentrop-Molotow, Interpretacje, mituy, rzeczywistosc*, Institut historii Polskiej Akaddemii Nauk, 2020

Mackintosh, M., *Stalin's Policy towards Eastern Europe, 1939-1948. The General Picture* s.j.

Madajczyk, C., *Die Okkupationspolitik Nazideutschlands in Poland 1939-1945*, Koln: Pahl -Rugenstein 1988

Maier, S., *Die instrumentalisierung der Erinnerung. Wie Russland und Polen die eigene Geschichte lenken*. 04-04-2022 website Akademie für politische Bildung

Maiski, I., *Memoiren eines sowjetischen Botschafters*. Berlin: Dietz Verlag 1973

Massenflucht aus Barcelona. Nationale Geschütze beschiessen die Stadt, In: *Baruther Anzeiger* 25.01.1939

Mertelsmann, O./Rahi-Tamm, A., Soviet Mass Violence in Estonia revisited, In: *Journal of Genocide Research* (2009) 11, June-September

Metri, M., *From the Rapallo Treaty to War in Ukraine: the Western Policy Towards Moscow-Berlin Relations*. Strategic Culture Foundation, April 15, 2021

Meyer,H.F., *Blutiges Edelweiss. Die 1.Gebirgs-Division im Zweiten Weltkrieg*. Berlin: Ch.Links Verlag 2008

Musial, B., *Stalin's Beutezug. Die Plunderung Deutschlands und der Aufstieg der Sovjetunion zur Weltmacht*, Berlin: List Verlag, 2011

Nazi-Soviet Conspiracy and the Baltic States. Diplomatic Documents and other Evidence. London: Boreas Publishing Co. 1948

O'Keeffe, B., *Madame comrade. How Ivy Litvinov, the English-born wife of a Soviet ambassador, seduced America with wit, tea and soft diplomacy*
Overy, R.,/Wheatcroft, A.,,. *The Road to War*, London: Vintage, 1989

Pätzold, K.,/Weissbecker, M., *Adolf Hitler. Eine politische Biographie*, Leipzig: Militizke Verlag 1995
Pierik, P.,/Reijmerink, M., Rechts lonkt naar de macht in Polen, In: *Algemeen Dagblad* 24.06.1993
Pierik, P., /Reijmerink, M., Lech Walesa speelt dubieuze rol in aanloop verkiezingen, In: *Haagsche Courant* 24.08.1993
Pierik, P., *Karl Haushofer en het nationaal-socialisme. Tijd, werk en invloed*, Soesterberg: Uitgeverij Aspekt 2006
Pierik, P., *De Poolse oorlog. Nieuwe feiten rond diplomatie, onderdrukking, oorlog, spionage en slachtofferschap*, Soesterberg: Uitgeverij Aspekt, 2021
Pierik, P., *Wapenbroeders. Romenië, nazi Duitsland en Operatie 'Barbarossa'*, Soesterberg: Uitgeverij Aspekt, 2021

Pierik, P., *Met Hitler voor moedertje Rusland. De geschiedenis van patriottisische Sovjetcollaborateurs*, Soesterberg: Uitgeverij Aspekt, 2022

Pierik, P., *Hitlers Lebensraum. De geestelijke wortels van de veroveringsveldtocht naar het oosten* (later reissued as *De geopolitiek van het Derde rijk*) Soesterberg: Uitgeverij Aspekt 1999

Polonsky,A., Stalin and the Poles 1941-7, In: *European History Quarterly* Vol. 17, 1987

Rabenau, F.von., (hg.), *Seeckt, Aus seinem Leben*, Leipzig: Von Hase&Koehler Verlag, 1941

Roberts, G., The Fall of Litvinov: A revisionist View. In: *Journal of Contemporary History* London/Newbury Park/New Delhi Vol. 27 1992

Rudling, P.A., The OUN , the UPA and the Holocaust. A Study in the Manufactering of historical Myths In: *The Carl Beck Papers in Russian & East European Studies* Number 2107 University of Pittsburgh z.j.

Schukow, G.K., *Erinnerungen und Gedanken*, Stuttgart: DVA 1969

Slutsch,S., 17.September 1939. Der Eintritt der Sowjetunion in den Zweiten Weltkrieg, In: *Vierteljahshefte für Zeitgeschichte, 2000, Heft 2.*

Soviet botschaft verliess Warschau. Durch deutsche Hilfe befreit. In: *Bayreuther Zeitung* 27.09.1939.

Stahl,F., *Heereseinteilung 1939*, Eggolsheim; Dorfler-Verlag z.j.

Sündermann, H., *Die Gezeichneten. Tatsachen* über *die Schuldigen des Zweiten Weltkrieges*. Berlin: Zentralverlag der NSDAP 1945,

Toland, J., *Hitler, Het einde van een mythe*, Utrecht: A.W.Bruna, 1983
Tschetschenenführer Kadyrov droht Poland mit Krieg. *Blue News* 27-05-2022

Vermaat, E., *Het Ribbentrop - Molotov Pact 1939. De prelude op de Tweede Wereldoorlog*, Soesterberg: Uitgeverij Aspekt, 2005

Weeks, A.L.*Stalin's other war. Soviet Grand Strategy 1939-1941*, p.85/Robert Conquest, *Stalin, Breaker of Nations*, London: Weidenfeld, 1993

Wat is Anti-Komintern? Niet 'Anti-Russisch' zegt Tokyo, In: *Algemeen Handelsblad voor Nederlandsch-Indië* 03.02.1940

Wheeler-Bennett, F.J.W., *The Nemesis of Power. The German Army in Politics 1918-1945*, London: Macmillan & Co LTD, 1954

Wynot, E.D. Jr., *World of Delusions and Disillusions: The National Minorities during World War II*, Cambridge University Press 20.11.2018

Archive material:

Ia. Notice: Am Generalkommando IV.A.K. 21.09.1039, GDIR: File; 500, Folge 12474, Act 65-0015

1.Gebirgsdivision -Kommandeur-An die Truppe ist Folgenden bekanntzugeben, den 22 September 1939, GDIR: Bestand 500, Findbuch 12474, Akte 272

56.Infantry Division, Div.St.Qu.Przemysl, 22.09.1939, GDIR: File 500, Findbuch 12477, Deed 446

213.I.D. Befehl für die Abriegelung des Gebietes beiderseits Kutno gegen flüchtende poln. Militar in Zivil, Div.St.Qu. den 18.09.1939, GDIR, file 500-Findbuch 12477, Akte 106-0106.

An die 10.Panzer Division, Bestand 500, Findbuch 12478-Akte b82-0020/10.Panzer-Divison Abt. Ia Div.St.Qu. den 24.09.1939: Betr: Zusammenstoss zwischen russ.Streitkräfte und der A.A. am 23.09.1939 Bestand 500, Findbuch 12478, Akte 82-0022

Armee Oberkommando 8 A.Gef.Stand Gradziek 27.09.1939 Armeebefehl NARA T354/R609.

Armeebefehl für die Herstellung u. Erhaltung der Ordnung in Bialystok, 18.09.1939 in: File 500, Folder 12472, Akte 151-0014

Ameekommando 14, Ia Nr. 131/39 A.H.Qu. Rzeszow

befehl 18.09.1939, GDIR Bestand 500-Findbuch 12477, Akte 446-0053
Bericht über das Zusammentreffen mit dem Russen zwischen Przemysel und Lemberg 26.09.1939 in: GDIR: File 500, Findbuch 12474, Akte 272-0214
Betr. Fernschreiben HZNH Nr. 186 HNCHG 1063 16.09. 12.40 Uhr. Secret! Mit richterlicher Untersuchung der Vorgänge in Bomberg Beauftragter Ob.Kriegsgerichtrat meldet: NARA T354/R609

Der Kommandierende General, Das XVIII.Armeekorps, Ermächtigung zu Verhandlungen mit der russischen Kommandostelle, 22.09.1939, GDIR: File 500, Findbuch 12474, Akte 272.
Der Oberbefehlshaber der Luftwaffe-Luftwaffe-Führungsstab Ic Lagebericht Ost nr.29, 17.09.1939 In: GDIR: File 500, Findbuch 12452, Akte 72
Der Oberbefehlshaber der Luftwaffe, Luftwaffe-Führungsstab Ic, Lagebericht Ost Nr. 32 20.09.1939, GDIR: Bestand 500, Findbuch 12452, Akte 77
Der Oberbefehlhaber der Luftwaffe, Luftwaffe-Führungsstab Ic, 19.09.1939 GDIR, Bestand 500, Findbuch 14252, Akte 77
Der Oberbefehlshaber der Luftwaffe-Luftwaffe-Führungsstab Ic Lagebericht Ost nr.29, 17.09.1939 In: GDIR: File 500, Findbuch 12452, Akte 72
Der Chef des Heeresnachrichtenwesens, Horchleitstelle,Nr. 2682/39g, Horchlage Ost, Berlin 21.09.1939, GDIR: File 500, Findbuch 12472, Akte 145-0015

Fernschreiben A.O.K.14 23.09.1939 File 500, Findbuch 12474, Akte 272-0260

Fernschreiben, Geheim 25.09.1939 GDIR: File 500 Findbuch 12464, Akte 83-0028.

Fernschreiben HDIH 884 an H.N.F.Allenstein und H.Gr.Nord 23/24.09,1939 GDIR: File 500, Findbuch 12459, Akte 29-0022.

Fernschreiven H.Gr.Nord -geheime Kommandosache 22.09.1939, GDIR: Bestand 500, Findbuch 12464, Akte 83-0034.e

Fernschreiben an H.Gr.Nord 17.09.1939 GDIR: Bestand 500 Findbuch 12459,Akte 20-0004. This order was passed down to company level, possibly beyond. See: (2.)Panzer Division, Divisionsbefehl (probably 18 September) GDIR: File 500, Findbuch 12478, Akte 15-0007

Fernschreiben an H.Gr.Nord /H.Gr.Süd 17.09.1939 GDIR: File 500, Findbuch 12459, Akte 20-0006

Final Report to National Council for Soviet and East European Research. Jan Gross, Russian Rule in Poland, 1939-1941, 14 July 1984

Geheim! Oberkommando der Wehrmacht, Nachrichtenblatt Wehrewirtschaft UdSSR Nr.1 25.08.1939, NARA T311/R244

Generalkommando XVI.A.K., Korpsbefehl 20.09.1939, NARA T354/R609.

Heeresgruppenkommando 3, Ubersicht der politische Lage, Berichtszeit 19. Und 20.08.1939, Bestand 500, Findbuch 12464, Akte 93

Heeres-Gruppenkommando 3, Ubersicht über die politische Lage, Berichtszeit 21 und 22.08.1939, Bestand 500, Findbuch 12464, Akte 92

Heeresgruppe Nord Auszug aus Fernschreiben OKH, Abt.Fremde Heere Ost 16.09.1939 In: GDIR page 62851

Heeresgruppenkommando 3, Ubersicht über die politische Lage Berichtzeit 17.08,.1939, abgeschlossen 18.08.1939 In: GDIR Bestand 500, Findbuch 12464, Akte 93

H.Gr.Nord, Allenstein 22.09.1939 23.00Uhr. GDIR: File 500, Findbuch 12459, Akte 24-0036.

H.Gr.Nord, Allenstein 22.09.1939 23.00Uhr. GDIR: File 500, Findbuch 12459, Akte 24-0036.

Horchabtlg.Nord, Funklagemeldung Nr.2 Königsberg 18.09.1939, GDIR: File 500, Findbuch 12459, Akte 28-0041

Kommandierende General des XXII.A.K., at Siedliska, Korpsbefehl 19.09.1939, GDIR: File 500, Findbuch 12478, Akte 15-0011

Kommandostab XVIII, Geheim! den 21.09.1939, GDIR: File 500, Findbuch 12474, Akte 272-0259

Korpskommando XVIII., Meldung über die Fühlingsnahme mit dem russischen Korpskommando bei Lemberg (Podborce) am 22.09.18.00 Uhr, GDIR: File

500, Findbuch 12474, Akte 272-0293
KTB AOK14, 17.09.1939 GDIR: File 500, Findbuch 12468, Akte 10-0029
KTB AOK 14, 19.-20.09.1939, GDIR Bestand 500, Findbuch 12468, Akte 10-0031, 0032
KTB AOK 14, Darstellung der Ereignisse, 22.09.1939, GDIR: Bestand 500, Findbuch 12468, Akte 10-0048
Kurze wehrwirtschaftliche Ubersichten (Ausland) GDIR Akte 9)/Ausarbeitung des Oberkommandos der Wehrmacht, Die Wehrwirtschaft der Republik Polen Teil 1 vom Juni 1939 GDOR Akte 26

Major i.G.Nagel, Ia. 206 Division, Div.St.Qu.Friedrichshof: betrf.: Beobachtungen bei Berührung mit russ.truppen 26.09.1939 GDIR: Bestand 500, Findbuch 12459, Akte 209
Major Schmidt, Telephonische Meldung, 06.10.1939, File 500 Findbuch 12474, Akte 272-0052

Nachrichten. Deutschl.-Sender 12.30 Uhr 24.09.1939, NARA T354/R609.

Oberkommando der Wehrmacht, Betr. Wehrwirtschaft Polen, Nachrichtenblatt Wehrwirtschaft Polen Nr. 3 11.08.1939 NARA T311/R244.
OKH Bericht in: Anlage KTB Heeresgruppe Süd, Kielce 21.09.1939, NARA T311/Roll244.
OKH-Heeresgruppe B, Beobachtungen über Kampfverfahren der frz.Truppe seit dem 16.9.39 In: GDIR Be-

stand 500-Findbuch 12454-Akte 3.

OKH PA/GZ No.145 17.09.1939 GDIR File 500, Findbuch 12459, Akte 20-0009

OKH, Geheim! Die militaerische Lage in Polen am 12.08.1939, NARA T311/R236. In a Lagebericht dated 17.08.1939

Office of the Historian. Foreign Relations of the United States, 1949, Eastern Europe: *The Soviet Union, Volume V* The Director of the Policy Planning Staff (Kennan) to the Counselor of the Department of State (Bohlen), Frankfurt, March 15 1949.

Rede des Vorsitzenden des Rates der Volkskommisare der S.S.S.R. Genossen Molotoff [written like this in original document] vom 17.09.1939, GDIR: Bestand 500, Findbuch 12459, Akte 20-0031

Uebersetzung des von einem russischen Flieger über Bialystock abgeworfenen Flugblattes, 17.09.1939, GDIR File 500, Findbuch 12459, Akte 20-0022

Internet links:

https://repozytorium.ukw.edu.pl/bitstream/handle/item/5611/Wojna%20polsko%20sowiecka%201939.pdf?sequence=1 HYPERLINK "https://repozytorium.ukw.edu.pl/bitstream/handle/item/5611/Wojna%20polsko%20sowiecka%201939.pdf?sequence=1&isAllowed=y"& HYPERLINK "https://repozytorium.ukw.edu.pl/bitstream/handle/item/5611/Wojna%20polsko%20sowiecka%201939.pdf?sequence=1&isAllowed=y"isAllowed=y

https://repozytorium.ukw.edu.pl/bitstream/handle/item/5611/Wojna%20polsko%20sowiecka%201939.pdf?sequence=1 HYPERLINK "https://repozytorium.ukw.edu.pl/bitstream/handle/item/5611/Wojna%20polsko%20sowiecka%201939.pdf?sequence=1&isAllowed=y"& HYPERLINK "https://repozytorium.ukw.edu.pl/bitstream/handle/item/5611/Wojna%20polsko%20sowiecka%201939.pdf?sequence=1&isAllowed=y"isAllowed=y

https://www.military.com/daily-news/2019/08/27/japan-strikes-north-how-battle-khalkhin-gol-transformed-wwii.html

https://repozytorium.ukw.edu.pl/bitstream/handle/item/5611/Wojna%20polsko%20sowiecka%201939.pdf?sequence=1 HYPERLINK "https://repozytorium.ukw.edu.pl/bitstream/handle/item/5611/Wojna%20polsko%20sowiecka%201939.pdf?sequence=1&isAllowed=y" HYPERLINK "https://repozytorium.

ukw.edu.pl/bitstream/handle/item/5611/Wojna%20 polsko%20sowiecka%201939.pdf?sequence=1 HYPERLINK "https://repozytorium.ukw.edu.pl/bitstream/handle/item/5611/Wojna%20polsko%20 sowiecka%201939.pdf?sequence=1&isAllowed=y" & HYPERLINK "https://repozytorium.ukw.edu.pl/ bitstream/handle/item/5611/Wojna%20polsko%20 sowiecka%201939.pdf?sequence=1&isAllowed=y"isAllowed=y" HYPERLINK "https://repozytorium. ukw.edu.pl/bitstream/handle/item/5611/Wojna%20 polsko%20sowiecka%201939.pdf?sequence=1&isAllowed=y" & HYPERLINK "https://repozytorium. ukw.edu.pl/bitstream/handle/item/5611/Wojna%20 polsko%20sowiecka%201939.pdf?sequence=1&isAllowed=y" HYPERLINK "https://repozytorium. ukw.edu.pl/bitstream/handle/item/5611/Wojna%20 polsko%20sowiecka%201939.pdf?sequence=1 HYPERLINK "https://repozytorium.ukw.edu.pl/bitstream/handle/item/5611/Wojna%20polsko%20 sowiecka%201939.pdf?sequence=1&isAllowed=y" & HYPERLINK "https://repozytorium.ukw.edu.pl/ bitstream/handle/item/5611/Wojna%20polsko%20 sowiecka%201939.pdf?sequence=1&isAllowed=y"isAllowed=y" HYPERLINK "https://repozytorium. ukw.edu.pl/bitstream/handle/item/5611/Wojna%20 polsko%20sowiecka%201939.pdf?sequence=1&isAllowed=y"isAllowed=y https://repozytorium.ukw.edu.pl/bitstream/handle/ item/5611/Wojna%20polsko%20sowiecka%201939.

pdf?sequence=1 HYPERLINK "https://repozytorium. ukw.edu.pl/bitstream/handle/item/5611/Wojna%20 polsko%20sowiecka%201939.pdf?sequence=1&isAllowed=y"& HYPERLINK "https://repozytorium. ukw.edu.pl/bitstream/handle/item/5611/Wojna%20 polsko%20sowiecka%201939.pdf?sequence=1&isAllowed=y"isAllowed=y

Abbreviations:

Abt	Abteilung
D	Division
Geb	Gebirgs
GDIR	Germandocsinrussia
Gr	Gruppe
H.	Heeresgruppe
Hrg.	Heeresgruppe
I	Infantry
NARA	National Archives
Poln	Polnish
Pz	Panzer
St	Stand
V	Vertrauens

Annex:

THE RADIO SPEECH OF THE CHAIRMAN OF THE SOVIET OF VOLKSCOMMISSARISTS OF THE U.S.S.R. CAMPAIGN V. M. MOLOTOV 17 SEPTEMBER 1939

Comrades! Citizens of our great country!

The events caused by the Polish-German war showed the internal and obvious incapacity and of the Polish state. The Polish ruling circles went bankrupt. All this happened in the shortest possible time.

It has been two weeks, and Poland has lost all its industrial centres, most major cities and cultural centres. There is also no more Warsaw as the capital of the Polish state. Nobody knows where the Polish government is. The people of Poland are at the mercy of fate through their bad luck. The Polish state and its government have effectively ceased to exist. Because of this situation, the agreements between the Soviet Union and Poland have ceased to exist.

A situation has arisen in Poland that requires the Soviet government to take special care of state security. Poland has become a suitable terrain for all kinds of accidents and surprises that could threaten the USSR. The Soviet government has remained neutral until recently. But due to the circumstances indicated, it can no longer remain neutral.

It is also impossible to demand from the Soviet government an indifferent attitude to the fate of the related Ukrainians and Belarusians living in Poland, peoples previously deprived of their civil rights and now completely abandoned. The Soviet government considers it a sacred duty to lend a helping hand to Ukrainian and Belarusian brothers living in Poland. In view of this, the USSR government handed over a note to the Polish ambassador in Moscow this morning, stating that the Soviet government has instructed the Red Army High Command to order troops to cross the border and take the lives and property of the people of western Ukraine and western Belarus under their protection.

The Soviet government also stated in this note that it simultaneously intended to take all measures to pull the Polish people out of the ill-fated war into which they had been plunged by their irrational leaders and give them the chance to live a peaceful life.

In the first days of September, when a partial appeal was sent to the Red Army in Ukraine, to Belarus and to the other four military districts, the situation in Poland was not clear and this appeal was treated as a precautionary measure. No one could have imagined that the Polish state would find itself so impotent and in such rapid disorder as has now occurred across Poland. However, since this disorder has become a reality, and Polish politicians are completely bankrupt and incapable of changing the situation in Poland, our Red Army, which has been greatly replenished by the recent reservist call-up, must fulfil the honourable task assigned to it. The government expresses the firm conviction that our Red Army of Workers and Peasants will once again show its fighting strength, consciousness and discipline that will bring it to new achievements, heroism and glory in carrying out its great liberating task.

At the same time, the Soviet government has issued a copy of the note addressed to the Polish ambassador to all governments with which the USSR maintains diplomatic relations, while declaring that the Soviet Union will pursue a policy of neutrality towards all these countries.

This defines our latest activities through foreign policy. The government also appeals to the citizens of the Soviet Union with the following statement. In connection with the calling up of reservists among our citizens, there was an effort to save more food and other goods for fear that a card system would be introduced in the area of supplies. The government deems it necessary to note that it does not intend to introduce a rationing system on products and manufactures, even though government measures triggered by external events will drag on for some time. I fear that only those who engaged in excessive purchases of food and goods and hoarded unnecessary stocks are exposed to danger in the form of spoilage. Our country is supplied with everything it needs and can do without rationing in supplies.

Our task now, a task of every labourer and peasant, a task of every worker and intellectual, is to work honestly and unselfishly at his post and thus offer help to the Red Army.

As for the soldiers of our glorious Red Army, I have no doubt that they will fulfil their duty to the fatherland - with honour and glory.

Peoples of the Soviet Union, all citizens of our country, soldiers of the Red Army and the Navy are united more than ever around the Soviet government, around our Bolshevik Party, around the great Soviet leader, around the wise Comrade Stalin, for new and still unprecedented achievements in industry and in the collective farms, for the new glorious victories of the Red Army on the battle fronts.

Source: Пропагандист и агитатор РККА. Орган политического управления РККА. 19, October 1939. Computer-aided draft translation by Pauli Kruhse.